# THE BEAR AT THE GATE

# AEI-Hoover
# policy studies

The studies in this series are issued jointly
by the American Enterprise Institute
for Public Policy Research and the Hoover
Institution on War, Revolution and Peace.
They are designed to focus on
policy problems of current and future interest,
to set forth the factors underlying
these problems and to evaluate
courses of action available to policymakers.
The views expressed in these studies
are those of the authors and do not necessarily
reflect the views of the staff, officers
or members of the governing boards of
AEI or the Hoover Institution.

# THE BEAR
# AT THE GATE

Chinese policymaking under Soviet pressure

Harold C. Hinton

American Enterprise Institute For Public Policy Research
Washington, D. C.

Hoover Institution on War, Revolution and Peace
Stanford University, Stanford, California

AEI-Hoover Policy Study 1, 1971

(AEI Special Analysis 21;
Hoover Institution Studies 31)

Library of Congress Catalog No. 78-187517

*Printed in United States of America*

For Kurt London

# Contents

# Introduction

As these words are written (late 1971), dramatic developments are occurring in the relations between the People's Republic of China (or Communist China, referred to hereafter as China) and the United States. The most dramatic to date has been President Nixon's announcement of July 15, 1971, that he would visit China, an event currently scheduled for February 21, 1972.

## Recent Developments

Behind this announcement lies an important and complex sequence of events, involving not only shifts in American policy toward China but also a major power struggle in China, as well as Peking's shifting preoccupations with the United States, the Soviet Union, and Japan. The Soviet aspect of Peking's concerns, and in particular the effects that growing Soviet pressures on China since the mid-1960s have had on Chinese policymaking, form the main subject of this study. It is a subject with important implications for American policy toward China, toward Asia as a whole, and toward the Soviet Union.

The main beneficiary of the recent power struggle in China is Premier Chou En-lai, the man with whom President Nixon is scheduled to negotiate when he visits Peking and who, as the American journalist Edgar Snow learned during his recent visit to China (August 1970-February 1971), has been virtually running the country for some time under Chairman Mao Tse-tung's general guidance. Evidently, Chou has wanted still greater personal authority and wider acceptance in Peking of his policies, one of the most important of which is a diplomatic opening to the United States partially designed to restrain the Soviet Union. Since late 1970, accordingly, Chou has moved, with

1

the support of Mao and some other elements of the Chinese leadership, against a number of possible rivals and opponents whom he has obscurely labeled "sham Marxists." [1]

By the summer of 1971, the principal remaining problem was Defense Minister Lin Piao. Lin was a formidable figure since he was not only Mao Tse-tung's announced heir, but also the senior member of the military establishment whose local leaders now control nearly all the provinces as a result of the Cultural Revolution. Handicapped by poor health and inferior political capabilities, however, Lin had been unable to prevent Chou from establishing a superior political base not only within the central leadership but even, it appears, among the provincial military elites. Lin was also weakened by his simplistic Maoist outlook, which rendered him less able than Mao himself, and certainly less able than Chou, to adjust to certain new realities—for example, the menacing Soviet military buildup that had begun about 1966 along China's northern borders. Lin apparently continued to favor the essentially outmoded concept, adopted by Mao in about 1960, of a simultaneous political struggle—with military overtones involving, if necessary, a "people's war" to repel a possible invasion of China—against *both* the American and the Soviet "superpowers." [2] His major colleagues including Mao and Chou, on the other hand, had become convinced since the Soviet invasion of Czechoslovakia that the Soviet menace, as well as other considerations, required that Peking establish a viable political relationship with the United States, the most effective potential counterweight to the Soviet Union. [3]

To those persons, including Lin, who have charged that a policy shift of such proportions constituted an abandonment of the struggle

---

[1] Cf. "Commemorate the Fiftieth Anniversary of the Communist Party of China," *People's Daily, Red Flag,* and *Liberation Army Daily,* July 1, 1971.

[2] Cf. his *Long Live the Victory of People's War!* Peking: Foreign Languages Press, 1965.

[3] In his speech on the occasion of the 1970 National Day celebrations, Lin referred to "social-imperialism" (i.e., the Soviet Union) and to war preparedness measures in China, both of them concepts offensive and even provocative to Moscow (New China News Agency dispatch, October 1, 1970). In his own speech on the same occasion, Chou used neither of these terms (New China News Agency dispatch, September 30, 1970). Lin's photograph appeared (for the last time in this place) with Mao's on the front page of the *People's Daily* on Army Day (August 1) 1971, and the editorial on the same occasion ("Commemorate August 1, Army Day," *People's Daily, Red Flag,* and *Liberation Army Daily,* August 1, 1971), presumably reflecting Lin's attitude, referred pointedly to "social-imperialism" and war preparedness.

against "imperialism," Chou has pointed to the anti-Japanese emphasis in Chinese propaganda since late 1969; and he has asserted that Japan is essentially "imperialist" and is in the process of becoming a more serious threat to China than is the United States—as it was a generation ago when China received American support in its struggle against Japanese invasion. China's opening to the United States, Chou apparently alleges, tends to split the United States from Japan and render the Japanese menace more manageable. In reality, Chou takes the Japanese menace less seriously than Chinese propaganda suggests.[4]

The chief immediate value to China of the opening to the United States is that it acts as a restraint on the Soviet Union. However, the latter is too dangerous a neighbor to be provoked unnecessarily by Chinese public statements to this effect. Not only Chinese statements but Chinese behavior as well appear to be influenced by concern over possible Soviet reaction. An important example is the cautious Chinese response, to date, to the 1971 crisis between India and Pakistan, China's informal ally; in this conflict, the Soviet Union clearly supports India, one sign of this support being the Soviet-Indian friendship treaty of August 9, 1971. Presumably Peking believes that the Soviet Union would put pressure on the Chinese border, if that were necessary, to deter Chinese intervention in the Indo-Pakistani dispute. In short, Chou has been rationalizing a policy on anti-Japanese grounds that he is actually pursuing more significantly on anti-Soviet grounds.

In mid-August 1971, Chou began a series of moves evidently aimed at Lin. These moves were made at a time when the Chinese domestic situation had become comparatively stable through the establishment of the new set of provincial level Communist party committees that replaced those destroyed during the Cultural Revolution (1966-1968),[5] and when the announcement of the forthcoming Nixon visit to Peking signalled the opening to the United States. An important article was

---

[4] One of the fullest and most important public statements of Chou's position on Japan may be found in his interview with James Reston (text in *New York Times,* August 10, 1971). In an interesting interview with a Yugoslav correspondent, on the other hand, Chou indicated that the alleged Japanese menace was not a matter of urgency (although Chinese propaganda and Chou's own statements often assert or imply that it is): ". . . the revival of Japanese militarism and the modernization of Japanese troops . . . require time" (Zagreb *Vjesnik,* August 28, 1971).

[5] The four last provinces to form such committees (Tibet, Szechuan, Ningsia, and Heilungkiang) did so between August 12 and 19, 1971; the completion of the list of committees was celebrated in a *People's Daily* editorial ("Our Party is Advancing Vigorously") on August 27, 1971.

published at that time that apparently originated with Chou, or at least reflected his current line, but it was attributed to Lin since it was said to have been written under the auspices of the provincial party committee of his native province, Hupei.[6] The central message was that China, when threatened by one "imperialist" adversary, should cooperate temporarily with a lesser adversary that was also at odds with the main enemy. This could be taken in either or both of two ways: as advocating cooperation with the United States against Japan, or as advocating cooperation with the United States against the Soviet Union—which since March 1969 has sometimes been labeled "social-imperialist" in Chinese propaganda. Whatever Chou may have intended, Moscow evidently understood the message as directed against itself: during the next three weeks, the Soviet press erupted in a series of high level anti-Chinese articles, one of which implicitly attacked Chou as the architect of an anti-Soviet Sino-American understanding.[7]

It is not clear whether Chou was genuinely alarmed by these articles or whether he merely drew from them an additional incentive and pretext for accelerating his efforts to eliminate Lin Piao and move to a position of greater security via a closer relationship with the United States and entry into the United Nations. Lin was, or at any rate could plausibly be accused of being, persona non grata in Moscow. He was Mao's proclaimed heir and, next to Mao, he was the most conspicuous Chinese exponent of a variety of concepts that were unacceptable to Moscow, including that of "people's war"; he was also a leading symbol of the "military psychosis" that Soviet propaganda alleged had been gripping China since the onset of the Cultural Revolution. From the extraordinary flurry of Soviet diplomatic activity then in progress in other areas, notably the four-power (United States, Soviet Union, Britain, and France) agreement on West Berlin, it appeared that Moscow might be tidying up unfinished business in order to devote greater attention to

---

[6] "Strong Weapon to Unite the People and Defeat the Enemy—Study 'On Policy,' " *People's Daily,* August 17, 1971.

[7] The most important of these articles were: S. Tikhvinsky, "Soviet-Chinese Relations: Supporters and Opponents of Their Improvement," *Pravda,* August 20, 1971; L. Kirichenko, "The Peking Leaders' Foreign Policy," *Za Rubezhom,* no. 34 (August 20-26, 1971); S. Yurkov, "An Unwise Policy," *Izvestia,* August 26, 1971; I. Aleksandrov, "The Slogans and Deeds of the Chinese Leadership," *Pravda,* September 4, 1971; Tass dispatch, September 6, 1971 (summarizing a Japanese press report regarding secret agreements allegedly reached by Chou and Kissinger; this charge was rebutted in a New China News Agency statement of September 8, 1971); G. Apalin, "Unsound Doctrine," *Izvestia,* September 9, 1971.

China and perhaps even to attack it.[8] The West Berlin agreement, which appeared to settle an issue that had preoccupied the Soviet Union for a generation, had been signed on September 3, 1971, the sixth anniversary of the publication of a well known tract by Lin expounding his version of "people's war" with strong anti-Soviet overtones.[9] Chou undoubtedly noted this fact, and may have used it against Lin in the course of intraparty debate. Might Moscow be freeing its hands in the West in order to increase its pressures on China for the purpose among others of getting revenge on Lin Piao, who had once been accused in the Soviet press of personal responsibility for the outbreak of Sino-Soviet border hostilities in March 1969?[10] Chou, apart from his personal political feud with Lin, may well have argued that Lin was endangering Chinese security through his unpopularity in Moscow, as well as through his opposition to the opening to the United States. If this line of argument were accepted, the obvious conclusion would be that Lin must go.

Having evidently lined up the necessary support, Chou began his final assault against Lin on September 11. Significantly, this was the second anniversary of the crucial talks on the Sino-Soviet border dispute between Chou and Soviet Premier Aleksei Kosygin, and may have carried the implication that, much as Chou had acted in 1969 to ensure against a Soviet attack on China by negotiating with Kosygin, so he was now working toward the same end by getting rid of Lin Piao as a preliminary to planning for the Nixon visit.

The details of the ensuing struggle in Peking are obscure, but it is clear that Chou won. He probably used against Lin the charges, among others, that Lin had been creating a "cult of personality" around himself that constituted disrespect to Mao (especially since Mao's own cult was being reduced at that time) and that Lin's political prominence threat-

---

[8] In addition to the West Berlin agreement, note the Crimean "summit conference" of August 2, 1971 (cf. R. Waring Herrick, "Soviet Camp Concerts Countermoves to China at Crimean Summit," *Radio Liberty Dispatch,* September 7, 1971); the Soviet-Indian friendship treaty (August 9, 1971); and such later developments as General Secretary Leonid Brezhnev's trip to Yugoslavia and Foreign Minister Andrei Gromyko's trip to the United States in late September 1971; and President Nikolai Podgorny's trip to India, Burma, and North Vietnam in early October 1971. The replacement of Marshal M. Zakharov, who had apparently opposed war with China (Christian Duevel, "Disarray Among the Soviet Marshals," *Radio Liberty Dispatch,* May 22, 1969), as Chief of Staff of the Soviet Armed Forces by Army General V. G. Kulikov (Tass dispatch, September 22, 1971) may also have aroused concern in Peking.

[9] See note 2.

[10] Konstantin Simonov, "Thinking Out Loud," *Pravda,* May 3, 1969.

5

ened to reverse the Maoist (and Communist) principle of party control over the armed forces. Lin and some of his military colleagues, certain of whom may have been citing an increased Soviet threat stemming from Peking's opening to the United States as a reason for increasing the defense budget, were evidently purged. This event was not announced, however, and steps were taken to make the outcome of the struggle appear ambiguous to the Chinese public and the outside world. Among the signs of the struggle were the September 12 crash in the Mongolian People's Republic (Outer Mongolia) of a Chinese aircraft carrying nine individuals of unrevealed identity (some of whom were probably trying to defect to the Soviet Union) and the unprecedented cancellation of the most spectacular features of the annual celebration of China's National Day (October 1) amid reports of increased Sino-Soviet border tension.[11] Among the indications of intense Soviet interest in the struggle in Peking were a suspension of Soviet anti-Chinese polemics, an informal emergency meeting of the ruling Soviet Party Politburo on September 27 (evidently on the subject of China),[12] and the September 30 announcement from Moscow of the air crash of September 12.[13]

On October 5 it was announced in Peking and Washington that President Nixon's assistant, Dr. Henry Kissinger, would visit Peking for the second time later in the month (the first visit had occurred in July) to prepare for the Nixon trip. Three weeks later, while Kissinger was in China, Peking was voted into the United Nations in lieu of Nationalist China. Presumably a regime that had just acquired a permanent seat on the United Nations Security Council and was scheduled to receive President Nixon in the near future was much less likely than before to be attacked by the Soviet Union, no matter how serious Moscow's concern over Peking's policies and over its growing nuclear power.

---

[11] The best analyses of the struggle that the writer has seen are by Tad Szulc in *New York Times,* September 22, 1971; Lee Lescaze in *Washington Post,* September 23, 1971; Selig S. Harrison in *Washington Post,* September 23, 1971; Tad Szulc in *New York Times,* September 23, 1971; Lee Lescaze in *Washington Post* September 25, 1971; Victor Zorza in *Washington Post,* September 28, 1971; Stanley Karnow in *Washington Post,* October 20, 1971; Lee Lescaze in *Washington Post,* November 5, 1971; Tillman Durdin in *New York Times,* November 6, 1971; Stanley Karnow in *Washington Post,* November 10, 1971; Tillman Durdin in *New York Times,* November 20, 1971; Stanley Karnow in *Washington Post,* November 27, 1971; and Tillman Durdin in *New York Times,* November 28, 1971. The reports of Sino-Soviet border tension originated in Peking and were reported mainly in the Japanese press (Kyodo [Tokyo] dispatch, September 22, 23, 1971).

[12] Hedrick Smith in *New York Times,* September 28, 1971.

[13] Tass dispatch, September 30, 1971.

## Purpose of the Study

The main purpose of this study is to describe the pressures exerted on China by the Soviet Union since the mid-1960s, to attempt an explanation of Soviet objectives, and to indicate the effects that the pressures have had on Chinese domestic and foreign policy. These effects are found to be real and significant, but by no means decisive in every aspect of Chinese policymaking. In many cases the major factor involved is the trend toward stabilization and normalization of Chinese domestic and foreign policy that has been in effect since the end of the Cultural Revolution, the stormy political campaign that Chairman Mao Tse-tung waged for two and a half years (spring 1966-autumn 1968) to regenerate the momentum of the Chinese Revolution. The study concludes with an analysis of the United States' past relationship to and future options regarding the Sino-Soviet dispute and of recent and future American policy toward China.

## Origins of the Sino-Soviet Dispute

Although this study focuses on a particular aspect of the Sino-Soviet dispute, namely, the territorial and military aspect, it may be helpful to indicate briefly what, in the writer's opinion, are the sources of the dispute as a whole.[14] The Chinese Communists were willing, for a variety of ideological and practical reasons, to play a subordinate and generally cooperative role in the Sino-Soviet relationship during Stalin's lifetime. After he died in 1953, however, that willingness began to evaporate, partly because Mao Tse-tung felt himself ideologically and politically superior to Stalin's successors as he had not to Stalin himself, and partly because the successors—Soviet Premier Nikita Khrushchev in particular—took initiatives that Peking found unacceptably adverse to its own interests. Peking's own reconstruction is that the latter tendency became acute at the time of the Soviet Twentieth Party Congress (February 1956), when Khrushchev vilified Stalin's memory and implied strongly that fear of war with the United States would make the Soviet Union cautious about supporting the interests of other Communist parties, the Chinese presumably included. During the next four years, an increasingly open Sino-Soviet debate got under way, mainly over the proper means of coping with the United States and of promoting revolution in the Third World (the underdeveloped non-Communist countries). There were also major differences of policy toward Taiwan, which Peking was

---

[14] For a list of works on Sino-Soviet relations, see Selected Bibliography.

eager to "liberate" so as to unite the country, and toward India. During this period, as is shown in Chapter 1, there began to be indications that Peking considered it had some sort of territorial claim against Moscow. Sensitive though this issue was, it would probably not have been raised by Peking if the general political relationship between China and the Soviet Union had not been deteriorating.

In 1960 Peking grew increasingly vocal in stating its case, and Khrushchev retaliated by withdrawing economic and military aid. Soon it became clear that Peking was presenting itself to the Communist world not merely as a rival but as a would-be successor to Moscow from the standpoint of ideological and political authority, and was trying to promote Khrushchev's overthrow. Khrushchev retaliated by attempting with little success to mobilize international Communist opinion to discipline the Chinese or at least isolate them. As the dispute grew increasingly bitter in 1963-1964, Peking raised the territorial issue in a much more open and serious way than it had in the 1950s. It was in this tense atmosphere that Khrushchev was overthrown (October 1964).

By that time, Soviet "revisionism" (a term indicating a deviation from Communist orthodoxy in a moderate direction) had become a target of Mao's wrath comparable to American "imperialism," and therefore a target of his domestic and foreign propaganda as well. Both forms of propaganda were necessary as a means of rationalizing Peking's policies and generating support for them. It was largely for this reason that Mao rejected, in late 1964 and early 1965, a proposal of Khrushchev's successors for a limited settlement of the Sino-Soviet quarrel. The dispute went on much as before, although within a changing context created by such major developments as the Cultural Revolution in China and the escalation of the Vietnam conflict in 1965. That conflict, which was the outgrowth of North Vietnam's determination to take over South Vietnam, had increasingly involved the United States, since 1949, in an effort to prevent the unification of Vietnam under Communist control. The escalation of 1965 was the result of American determination to frustrate Hanoi's effort to take over South Vietnam by sending regular North Vietnamese troops into the south.

**The Border Issue**

One manifestation of recent Chinese policy that can be attributed directly to Soviet pressure is the Sino-Soviet talks that began in October 1969 on the territorial dispute between the two parties. The origins and development of this dispute and the progress of the talks are analyzed in some detail in this study.

For several months before the beginning of the talks, war had appeared imminent. Moscow had built up its forces near the Chinese border and threatened Peking with an invasion, a nuclear strike, or both, unless the Chinese agreed to hold talks on the border issue and on the normalization of state-to-state relations between China and the Soviet Union. In the sense that the Soviet Union threatened to attack and refrained, this crisis resembled the one involving Romania and the Soviet Union in the summer of 1968. There were important differences, however. Romania had retained the orthodox Leninist principle of rule by the Communist party apparatus, which China had jettisoned at least temporarily during the Cultural Revolution. This principle is one about which Moscow cares deeply; its weakening in Czechoslovakia in 1968 had been a major cause of the Soviet invasion of that country. Romania had no open territorial dispute with the Soviet Union; China had. Romania took care not to provoke the Soviet Union along their common border while it was preparing to fight a "people's war" if necessary; China committed a major military provocation of the Soviet Union along the border and only then, alarmed by Moscow's response, began to prepare for a "people's war." Romania received declaratory support from the United States; China did not. Both China and Romania considered it advisable to supplement their preparations for defense with indication of willingness to negotiate and indeed to make substantive concessions.

China's performance under Soviet pressure in 1969 was marked by great boldness up to what it believed to be the brink of war, by a constant recalculation of the risks, and by a willingness to retreat when necessary. The same skill at crisis management, combined with occasional rashness in initiating crises, can be seen at intervals throughout the history of China's foreign policy since the Communist seizure of power in 1949.

### Essentials of Chinese Foreign Policy

Underlying the phenomena discussed in this introduction and to be discussed in the main body of the study are the basic characteristics of Chinese foreign policy. A brief summary of this complex subject may be helpful.[15]

---

[15] These themes have been developed at greater length by the writer in *Communist China in World Politics,* Boston: Houghton Mifflin, 1966; and *China's Turbulent Quest,* New York: Macmillan, 1970.

Chinese foreign policy displays, usually in combination rather than separately, both national (Chinese) and ideological (Communist) traits corresponding to the Peking leadership's ambition to make China both a major Asian (and eventually a world) power and a worldwide revolutionary influence. The proportions of national and ideological elements vary according to the time and situation; rarely is either category entirely absent.

Like every other national leadership, China's is preeminently concerned to ensure the security of its country and regime. Like many others, it often tends to exaggerate the seriousness of a particular threat and accordingly to overreact. In the Chinese case, such exaggeration is more understandable than in some others, since China was victimized by various foreign powers, Japan above all, for the greater part of the century prior to the end of the Second World War in 1945. Peking is sensitive to the perils of the nuclear age, which it believes, however, can usually be avoided through proper political strategy and tactics; on occasion, as at the end of the Korean War in 1953, Peking has tacitly capitulated to a virtual nuclear ultimatum—American in that case—in order to ensure survival. Peking's growing nuclear capability is presumably designed partially to eliminate the necessity for more such retreats in the future.

At a less dramatic level, Peking is hypersensitive to any semblance of a military threat to its frontiers or border regions, and it regards the presence of any strong hostile force near its borders as constituting such a threat. It has reluctantly accepted a strong Soviet military presence to the north, since the Soviet Union was Peking's major ally, at first, after 1949; in any case, Peking had no effective choice in view of Russia's long history as an Asian territorial power and its obvious determination to remain one. But Peking has not accepted passively the presence of the forces of other powers in the immediate vicinity of its frontiers. Although the theory of Maoist "people's war" holds that China should "lure the enemy to penetrate deeply" into its territory the better to annihilate him, in practice China has behaved more like a conventional state in such cases, sometimes to the point of launching some form of preemptive or spoiling attack when it felt unduly threatened. The classic example of such behavior is Peking's intervention in the Korean War late in 1950, with the main purpose of rolling General Douglas MacArthur's forces back from the Manchurian frontier. As a result of this intervention, Peking also preserved North Korea—which MacArthur had been trying to annex to South Korea by force following the unsuccessful invasion of South Korea by North Korea in June 1950—as a Communist state, as well as a buffer for China.

The second major category of Chinese foreign policy objectives relates to influence. Under this heading domestic and external behavior are closely linked. Peking cultivates the intense nationalism of the educated Chinese public for purposes of political mobilization through the concentration of hostile propaganda on some external "negative example," or in other words an adversary real or alleged. In the process, not only can domestic tensions be projected outward to some extent rather than focusing on the regime itself, but the extensive latent sympathy for China in other countries can be exploited.

Among the issues that Peking has tried to use for these purposes is the pre-1945 seizure by foreign "imperialist" states of territory considered by Peking as belonging to China. In general, Peking apparently does not seriously intend to make a claim for the restoration of these territories, but it does not wish to lose the benefit of the issue at home and abroad by making this attitude explicit. The exceptions to this generalization, however, are interesting and significant. Peking's position—that the treaties under which tsarist Russia acquired territory from the Manchu empire in the Far East and Central Asia are "unequal" and therefore invalid—contributed heavily to the Sino-Soviet crisis of 1969. Soviet pressure has compelled Peking to make it clear, since April 1969, that China makes no formal claim for the restoration of territory lost under these "unequal" treaties. In other cases, similar claims have been kept alive at least by implication, unless they could be traded away, wholly or in part, in territorial settlements. Peking has concluded such settlements formally—and usually on the basis of reasonable compromise—with Burma (1960), Nepal (1960), the Mongolian People's Republic (1962), Afghanistan (1963), and informally with North Korea. Territorial settlements remain to be concluded with the Soviet Union and India; Peking's relations with both of them are too bad at present to permit such a settlement.

A different attitude exists toward territory that Peking regards as having been detached from China's control, or imminent control, since the end of the Second World War. One such case is the Mongolian People's Republic (Outer Mongolia), to which Peking feels it has some sort of claim even though Mongolia has been a Soviet dependency since 1921, had declared itself independent of China in 1945, was recognized

11

by Peking in 1949, and in Peking's eyes has been occupied by Soviet forces for anti-Chinese purposes since about 1966. The other such case is Taiwan, which Peking considers it was prevented from "liberating" from Nationalist control only because the United States "occupied" it—actually, took it under protection—in 1950. Although Peking's claim to the Mongolian People's Republic may not be entirely serious, its claim to Taiwan certainly is, if only because Taiwan is the seat of a rival government. Pending the "liberation" of Taiwan, the issue serves Peking well in the mobilization of domestic and external support.

Both for the purpose of enhancing its influence and in the hope of resolving particular issues on its own terms, Peking has conducted political struggles, with strong military aspects at times, against a succession of foreign adversaries. The major adversaries have been, in chronological order of the beginning of the quarrel at a serious level, the United States (from 1950), India (from about 1959), the Soviet Union (from about 1960), and Japan (from about 1969). It is of course in connection with the struggle against the Soviet Union that, as already indicated, Peking has laid claim to ideological and political primacy within the international Communist movement. So heavily has Chinese foreign policy been preoccupied with these disputes that Peking has chosen its foreign friends to a considerable extent from among those countries opposed to its adversaries and has cultivated them for the purpose of waging a common political struggle against the adversary in question.

Although Peking aspires to make China a true world power in the long run, a major medium-term objective—one falling more under the heading of national interest than of ideology—is to achieve primacy in Asia, not necessarily in military power but certainly in political influence. Peking hopes ultimately to be at the head, but not necessarily in full control, of a system of Asian Communist states to whose revolutions China will have given indispensable political support and perhaps military aid (probably without direct intervention). In the meantime, China employs conventional diplomatic methods and international tactics to enhance its influence in Asia, in addition to supporting revolution where feasible.

Finally, and more under the heading of ideology than of national interest, Peking tries to give inspiration and leadership to leftist revolutionary movements—by no means all of them Communist in the usual sense—in the Third World, in the West, and in the Soviet-oriented Communist countries. This tendency is a fundamental characteristic of Maoist ideology, although it may be subordinated to considerations of national interest in particular cases when Peking has some reason for wanting to cultivate the established government of the country in question and therefore to avoid working for its overthrow.

Peking's actual behavior in external crises has often appeared to be motivated by combinations of the considerations just discussed, particularly by the considerations of internal mobilization, security, and international prestige. This was conspicuously true of the three major crises in which Peking became involved before its relations with the Soviet Union deteriorated to the point of direct confrontation. These crises were the Sino-American war in Korea (1950-1953), the Taiwan Strait crisis of 1958 (which Peking initiated to promote the great internal political campaign known as the Great Leap Forward, to move toward the "liberation" of Taiwan by driving a wedge between the Chinese Nationalists and their American allies, and to galvanize Khrushchev into adopting a more resolutely anti-American stand), and the Sino-Indian border war of 1962 (which Peking initiated to push the Indian Army farther from the borders of turbulent Tibet and to humiliate the detested Nehru government).

The same combination of major considerations—internal mobilization, security, and international prestige—can be seen at work in Peking's management of its crisis with the Soviet Union that began after the Soviet invasion of Czechoslovakia in 1968. In the writer's opinion, this latest crisis, between China and the Soviet Union, is fully comparable in importance and interest to the three great earlier ones. And we have not yet necessarily seen the end of it.

# 1

# Origins and Development of Soviet Pressures on China

## The Border Issue as an Element of the Sino-Soviet Dispute

A major cause of the rapid deterioration in Sino-Soviet relations after the mid-1950s was Moscow's concern at the growth of Maoist nationalism—one manifestation of which was Chinese rejection of the territorial losses inflicted on the Chinese Empire in the nineteenth century through "unequal" treaties imposed by the imperial powers of that era, tsarist Russia included.[1] Russia had pushed back the Manchurian frontier to the Amur and Ussuri rivers by the treaties of Aigun (1858) and Peking (1860) and had fixed the border between Sinkiang (Chinese Turkestan) and Russian Central Asia by the Treaty of Ili (1881).

In October 1954 and January 1957—times of political difficulty for Khrushchev—Peking exacerbated the situation by raising in secret discussions the question of the post-1917 territorial status of the Mongolian People's Republic; the Soviet Union had effectively detached that republic from Chinese sovereignty and made it into a client state of its own during the 1920s.[2]

From Moscow's point of view, discussions on territorial questions were likely to lead to formal demands for restoration of the lost terri-

---

[1] For an excellent discussion of China's border problems and policy see Guy Searls, "Communist China's Border Policy: Dragon Throne Imperialism?" *Current Scene* (Hong Kong), vol. ii, no. 12 (April 15, 1963). On the background of the Sino-Soviet border dispute see Peter Berton, "Background to the Territorial Issue," *Studies in Comparative Communism,* vol. 2, nos. 3 and 4 (July/October 1969), pp. 131-148.

[2] See the Chinese statements on these episodes quoted in the valuable compilation edited by Dennis J. Doolin, *Territorial Claims in the Sino-Soviet Dispute: Documents and Analysis,* Stanford University: Hoover Institution Studies 7, 1965, pp. 43, 45-46.

tories, a possibility totally unacceptable to the Soviet Union, as indeed it would be to virtually any state in a comparable situation.[3] Maoist nationalism was bound to evoke, through a natural reactive process, a display of Soviet anti-Chinese nationalism, a phenomenon that the Soviet Union's superior strategic military power rendered a dangerous one for Peking.

In January 1959 Peking worsened its relations with India, and indirectly its relations with the Soviet Union, by formally repudiating the McMahon Line (the eastern sector of the Sino-Indian border claimed by India since 1914) as an imperialist fabrication imposed on China in the days of its weakness, and therefore invalid.[4] Since the Sino-Soviet border rested on similarly drawn lines, Moscow can hardly have failed to be disturbed. There is unpublished evidence from Soviet sources that later in 1959, when border hostilities arose between Chinese and Indian troops, Soviet forces in Central Asia mobilized near the Sinkiang frontier with the aim of relieving Chinese pressures on India.[5] And a Soviet statement of September 9, 1959, implicitly blamed the Chinese side for the tension along the Sino-Indian frontier.[6]

After 1961 the Soviet Union began to reinforce its military posture in Central Asia and the Far East.[7] This process was probably accelerated by tension along the Sinkiang border in the spring of 1962; Peking's version of this action is that the Soviet Union incited thousands of

---

[3] In his memoirs (assuming them to be authentic) Khrushchev says that (apparently at some time between 1958 and 1964) the Chinese "sent us their version of how the map should read. We took one look at it, and it was so outrageous that we threw it away in disgust." (Edward Crankshaw ed., *Khrushchev Remembers,* Boston: Little, Brown and Co., 1970, p. 474.)

[4] Letter of January 23, 1959, from Chou En-lai to Nehru (text in *Notes, Memoranda and Letters Exchanged and Agreements Signed Between the Governments of India and China, 1954-1959: White Paper,* Ministry of External Affairs, New Delhi, n.d. [1959], pp. 52-54).

[5] Wayne Wilcox, "China's Strategic Alternatives in South Asia," in Tang Tsou, ed., *China's Policies in Asia and America's Alternatives,* University of Chicago Press, 1968, p. 415.

[6] Peking later called this statement "the first instance in history in which a socialist country, instead of condemning the armed provocations of the reactionaries of a capitalist country, condemned another fraternal socialist country when it was confronted with such armed provocations" ("Whence the Differences?" *People's Daily,* February 27, 1963).

[7] Cf. William Whitson's statement in *United States-China Relations: A Strategy for the Future,* Washington: U.S. Government Printing Office for the House Committee on Foreign Affairs, 1970, p. 144.

disaffected tribesmen to flee from Sinkiang into Soviet Central Asia.[8]

In December 1962 Khrushchev, enraged by what he considered insulting and provocative Chinese criticism of the Soviet response to the Cuban missile crisis, publicly denounced Peking. Khrushchev asked why, now that China had taken successful military action (in October-November 1962) against India over the Sino-Indian border dispute, it did not react similarly over formerly Chinese areas, such as Hong Kong, which were under the control of the relatively strong "imperialist" powers.[9] Peking had been engaged since 1960 in trying with some success to isolate India and the Soviet Union from possible sources of support on the border question by negotiating boundary treaties with some of its other neighbors (Mongolia, Burma, Nepal, Pakistan, and Afghanistan). But Peking was not content with positive measures of this kind and, ignoring Khrushchev's taunt, waited until he had been echoed by the Communist Party of the United States and then indicated in a statement published on March 8, 1963, that the "unequal" treaties imposed on China by "imperialism," including those signed with tsarist Russia, might have to be reexamined and renegotiated.[10]

It was now clear that the Sino-Soviet border issue required formal attention by the two parties. In accordance with a Soviet proposal to Peking of May 1963, talks at the deputy foreign minister level began in Peking in February 1964. The two sides agreed that a new boundary treaty was desirable and that minor adjustments in particular places, mainly riverine islands, needed to be made. But Peking, then on the political offensive against Khrushchev, insisted that the Soviet Union accept and incorporate in the new treaty several particulars: the Chinese contentions that the old treaties were invalid because of their "unequal" character, that the Soviet Union in some places had gone beyond the border established by the "unequal" treaties, and that in the case of border rivers (the Amur and the Ussuri) the boundary should follow the main channel. The Soviet side refused to admit the unequal character of the old treaties, insisted that the main purpose of the new treaty

---

[8] See the passage from "The Origin and Development of the Differences Between the Leadership of the CPSU and Ourselves," *People's Daily* and *Red Flag,* September 6, 1963, quoted in Doolin, *op. cit.,* pp. 31-32.

[9] Quoted in *ibid.,* pp. 27-28. There is an obvious possibility that the timing of the Chinese border offensive against India was determined at least in part by the knowledge that the Soviet Union was preoccupied with the crisis over Cuba.

[10] "A Comment on the Statement of the Communist Party of the U.S.A.," *People's Daily,* March 8, 1963 (excerpts in Doolin, *op. cit.,* pp. 29-31).

was to confirm the status quo in its essentials, and rejected the main channel as the basis for the riverine boundary; it favored instead the Manchurian bank, as indicated on an old, small-scale map.

The talks were suspended after August 1964, apparently because of the fall of Khrushchev, and perhaps also because of an interview given by Mao Tse-tung on July 10 to a visiting Japanese delegation.[11] During the interview, Mao said that the Soviet Union had wrongfully taken territory from China and Japan and also from some European countries since the end of the Second World War, seeming to imply that the victims should cooperate politically with Peking in order to regain their lost territories.[12] The Soviet reply was an editorial published on September 2 (V-J Day) which implicitly threatened China with the fate of the Japanese Empire, or in other words military defeat, if it persisted in seeking territorial revision.[13]

The fall of Khrushchev did little to alleviate Sino-Soviet tension. In 1965 the two adversaries projected their antagonism mainly against the backdrop of the struggle over Vietnam.

Moscow's bill of particulars against Peking as of early 1966 was presented—with the major omission of the recent crushing of a Communist coup in Indonesia—in a secret letter circulated among other parties regarded as more "fraternal" than the Chinese.[14] The occasion that induced the letter was Peking's rejection, in an editorial published the previous November 11,[15] of the Soviet proposal for some form of "united action" on behalf of North Vietnam. Peking was also alleged not only to have refused overflight rights for Soviet aircraft carrying military equipment for Hanoi but to have violated an agreement of April 1965 by obstructing the passage of similar equipment by rail.

Moscow also expressed its concern over a series of Chinese statements, notably one by Foreign Minister Chen Yi in a press conference of September 29, 1965,[16] on the likelihood of a Sino-Soviet war. China

---

[11] For a careful analysis of these talks see Thomas W. Robinson, *The Sino-Soviet Border Dispute: Background, Development, and the March 1969 Clashes,* The RAND Corporation, RM-6171-PR, August 1970, pp. 11-16.

[12] Quoted in Doolin, *op. cit.,* pp. 42-44.

[13] Quoted in *ibid.,* pp. 47-57.

[14] Text in "Geheime Anklageschrift Moskaus gegen Peking," *Ost-Probleme,* vol. 18, no. 8 (April 22, 1966), pp. 228-237.

[15] "Refutation of the New Leaders of the CPSU on 'United Action,'" *People's Daily* and *Red Flag,* November 11, 1965.

[16] See *Vice-Premier Chen Yi Answers Questions Put by Correspondents,* Peking: Foreign Languages Press, 1966, p. 24.

was said to have tried, during its massive propaganda campaign against Moscow, to turn the abortive Afro-Asian Conference—which was to have been held at Algiers in 1965 as the successor to the Bandung Conference of 1955—into an anti-Soviet forum and to have refused a Soviet request to follow a common policy toward the Indo-Pakistani war of August-September 1965. Peking had set up anti-Soviet "fractions" (splinter parties) in some thirty countries.

As for more ideological issues, Moscow accused Peking of having created a "cult of personality" around Mao Tse-tung and of having violated Leninist norms of party life. Peking allegedly had also taken a dangerously favorable attitude toward international tension and war, even nuclear war. Defense Minister Lin Piao's recent tract on "people's war" [17] had denied the leading revolutionary role to the international working class by counterposing the "world countryside" (the developing countries) against the "world city" (the developed countries). Peking had placed excessive emphasis on "armed struggle" as a revolutionary instrumentality. At the same time it had underestimated the significance of the construction of "socialism" and "communism" within the "socialist camp" for world revolution; and rather than supporting the "patriotic and revolutionary-democratic" forces said to be in power in some countries, it had worked for their overthrow.

This behavior on Peking's part, the secret letter concluded, had led to the rejection of an offer by Soviet Secretary General Leonid I. Brezhnev in November 1964 on a far-reaching accommodation in both the party and the state spheres. China was helping the United States in Vietnam and elsewhere, and it also was complicating the task of convening another international conference of Communist parties like the one of 1960.

Later in 1966 even these important issues were largely submerged by the eruption in China of the Cultural Revolution. This was a phenomenon of immense concern to Moscow, since it produced the virtual annihilation in China of the orthodox Leninist principle of Communist party apparatus rule. An important aspect of Maoist behavior during the Cultural Revolution was an intense hostility toward the Soviet Union and toward Soviet nationals in China, an almost equally intense hostility toward the pro-Soviet leadership of the Mongolian People's Republic, and occasionally violent demonstrations by Red Guards (Maoist stu-

---

[17] Lin Piao, *Long Live the Victory of People's War!* Peking: Foreign Languages Press, 1965.

dents) and Chinese soldiers and peasants along and sometimes across the Sino-Soviet border.

The Soviet response to these developments included not only a propaganda campaign against Mao Tse-tung and the Cultural Revolution but other measures more directly related to the Sino-Soviet border issue. Soviet broadcasts incited disaffection among the minority peoples of Sinkiang. The Soviet military buildup in areas near the Chinese border, including Mongolia, was accelerated. During 1966, and especially at the time of the December Plenary Session of the CPSU Central Committee, the Soviet leadership appears to have given serious consideration to some form of military intervention in China. If so, it obviously decided in the end to refrain, probably because no political base, such as an anti-Maoist coalition that might have been willing to accept Soviet support, appeared, even to the limited extent that a pro-Soviet base for intervention existed in Czechoslovakia in August 1968.[18]

## Escalation of the Sino-Soviet Border Dispute

In view of the strength of Soviet objections to the Cultural Revolution in general and the Red Guards in particular, it is surprising that the suppression of the Red Guards by the army at Mao's direction and the end of the Cultural Revolution in the late summer and early autumn of 1969 were followed by an increase rather than a decrease in Sino-Soviet tension over the border issue. There are several reasons for this apparent anomaly.

One of the most important is the official Soviet assessment of the outcome of the Cultural Revolution as a "military-bureaucratic dictatorship"—a dictatorship controlled by Mao and the most Maoist elements of the military leadership, especially Defense Minister Lin Piao, exercised through the provincial revolutionary committees, and scheduled for legitimation at the forthcoming Ninth Party Congress.[19] Any Soviet leader who subscribed to this assessment would be likely to expect the worst from the domestic and foreign [20] policies of such a regime, and

---

[18] The Cultural Revolution period in Sino-Soviet Relations is well analyzed in Maury Lisann, "Moscow and the Chinese Power Struggle," *Problems of Communism,* vol. xviii, no. 6 (November-December 1969), pp. 32-41.

[19] Cf. O. Lvov (pseud.), "The Political Maneuvers of the Mao Tse-tung Group," *Pravda,* January 11, 1969.

[20] Cf. G. Apalin, " 'New Period' in Peking's Foreign Policy?" *International Affairs* (Moscow), no. 2 (February 1969), pp. 7-13.

might plausibly conclude that the only hope of improving its behavior lay in pressure of one kind or another.[21]

A number of more specific factors heightened Soviet objections to Chinese policy during the early post-Cultural Revolution period.

From the Soviet point of view, Chinese behavior during the East European crisis of 1968 had been distinctly provocative. Following the invasion of Czechoslovakia, Peking had proclaimed "support" for the "people" (although not for the "revisionist leading clique") of Czechoslovakia and for Romania, Yugoslavia, and Albania, all three of which also appeared to be threatened to some degree.[22] On August 21, the day of the invasion, Peking for the first time gave public approval to the pro-Chinese "Communist Party of Poland." [23] Of particular importance to Peking was the fate of Albania, its closest and indeed its only East European friend. A Chinese statement of September 16 alleging Soviet flights over Chinese territory during August was probably aimed at distracting Soviet attention from Albania's withdrawal from the Warsaw Pact on September 12.[24] Two days later Mao Tse-tung, Lin Piao, and Chinese Premier Chou En-lai sent a message to the Albanian leadership indicating their support for the "East European peoples in their just struggle against the Warsaw Treaty Organization, which is controlled by Soviet revisionism." [25] At the end of September an Albanian delegation led by Defense Minister Bequir Balluku visited China (including Sinkiang on the Sino-Soviet border), and two months later Chinese Chief of Staff Huang Yung-sheng returned the visit. At about that time there were reports, to Moscow's distress,[26] of significant increases in the flow of

21 The long anti-Maoist tirade by a former rival of Mao's now resident in Moscow, Wang Ming (*China: Cultural Revolution or Counter-Revolutionary Coup?* Moscow: Novosti, 1969, originally published in the *Canadian Tribune,* March 19, 1969) could be considered a case of political pressure exerted, although ineffectively, shortly before the opening of the Ninth Congress.

22 See, e.g., speeches by Chou En-lai of August 23 and September 30, 1968 (texts released by New China News Agency on dates of delivery). On the intensification of Chinese radio propaganda to Eastern Europe at this time see Bernard Gwertzman in *New York Times,* September 26, 1968.

23 Cf. j.c.k. (Joseph C. Kun), "Chinese Endorsement of Pro-Peking Polish CP," Radio Free Europe Research Paper, September 20, 1968.

24 Chinese statement of September 16, 1968 (text released by New China News Agency, same date).

25 Text released by New China News Agency, September 18, 1968.

26 Cf. V. Shelepin, "Albania in Peking's Plans," *New Times* (Moscow), no. 7 (February 19, 1969), pp. 19-20.

Chinese economic and military aid to Albania. There were even rumors that Chinese naval and missile bases were to be established in Albania.[27]

During 1968 serious tension existed in the Sino-Soviet border region. The fall of Ulanfu, the Mongol boss of the Inner Mongolia Autonomous Region, in the spring of 1967 during the Cultural Revolution in that area, had created serious turmoil that had aroused concern in the Mongolian People's Republic.[28] By mid-1968, Mongolian officials in Ulan Bator were privately expressing alarm over the possibility of a Chinese invasion of the Mongolian People's Republic.[29] Sino-Soviet tension over Sinkiang was indicated by occasional Chinese references to Soviet efforts to "subvert" the area,[30] and was probably heightened by the removal of Wang En-mao, the erstwhile boss of the region, in the autumn of 1968 and by the testing of a Chinese thermonuclear device over Lop Nor on December 28.

From the Chinese point of view, the invasion of Czechoslovakia and the subsequent proclamation of the Brezhnev Doctrine stating that the Soviet Union has the right to intervene in Communist countries to preserve the "socialist system" had been alarming. Was China next on the Soviet target list? There were reasons to fear that it might be so. From mid-December 1968 to early February 1969, Soviet Premier Aleksei Kosygin was absent from his duties, probably because of illness, and during this period the ascendancy in the Kremlin evidently passed to a "hawkish" faction centering on Brezhnev; this faction favored a confrontation with China, partly in order to create an issue that would help to rally the Warsaw Pact states under Soviet leadership.[31] A number of bellicose statements were published in the Soviet press during this period, apparently as a reflection of the "minicrisis" then building up over West Berlin, but also no doubt for effect on Peking. The Chinese aspects were especially clear in a menacing article on the Brezhnev

[27] *The Observer* (London), December 8, 1968.

[28] Cf. Paul Hyer, "The China-Mongol Frontier: The Cultural Revolution and After," a paper presented at the First Sino-American Conference on Mainland China, Taipei, Taiwan, December 1970.

[29] Personal information from a foreign diplomat who visited Ulan Bator at that time.

[30] See, e.g., speech by Saifudin, September 6, 1968 (text released by New China News Agency, same date).

[31] Cf. Christian Duevel, "A Volley of 'Hawkish' Lenin Quotations," *Radio Liberty Dispatch,* March 17, 1969.

Doctrine that appeared in *Red Star* on February 14, the anniversary of the signing of the Sino-Soviet alliance.[32]

Peking must have been still more alarmed when words turned into action. Intensified Soviet patrolling was initiated along the Far Eastern sector of the Sino-Soviet frontier, accompanied by a change in the rules of engagement which apparently permitted Soviet forces for the first time to fire on Chinese troops found on territory claimed by the Soviet Union, instead of trying to eject them by less violent means. According to a later Chinese statement, this change occurred after mid-February 1969;[33] according to another source, it took effect on March 2.[34] The area most affected comprised the numerous disputed islands in the Ussuri River which, because they were claimed by both sides, had already been the scene of a number of nonlethal encounters between Soviet and Chinese patrols. This Soviet initiative, which was not technically of an aggressive character and may have fallen short of what was desired by the "hawks," probably reflected the effect of Kosygin's return to the Politburo. It may well have been intended to deter anticipated Chinese efforts to intensify border tension, through local incidents short of war, as a means of creating an appropriately militant atmosphere for the long-delayed Ninth Party Congress, which at that time seemed likely to open in mid-March. If, in addition, the proceedings of the congress could be influenced in the direction of moderation, so much the better. The islands were a convenient arena because the impending thawing of the ice and their remoteness from the most sensitive sectors of the Sino-Soviet frontier, such as the Mongolian and Sinkiang borders, limited the likelihood of unwanted escalation.

From Peking's perspective, it may have appeared that the Soviet Union was contemplating direct military action to affect or even preempt the Ninth Party Congress, much as the Soviet invasion of Czechoslovakia had been designed partially to forestall the Fourteenth Party Congress. Also, in Chinese eyes, the Soviet decision not to press the Berlin "mini-crisis" vigorously may have foreshadowed a disengagement in the West in order to engage in the East.[35] Be that as it may, Peking decided

---

[32] Maj. Gen. K. Bochkarev, "V. I. Lenin and the Defense of the Achievements of Socialism: The Great International Duty," *Red Star,* February 14, 1969.

[33] Chinese note to Soviet Union of May 24, 1969 (text released by New China News Agency, same date).

[34] Paul Wohl in *Christian Science Monitor,* June 2, 1969.

[35] Cf. Albert Boiter, "The Berlin Mini-Crisis of 1969: A Backgrounder," *Radio Liberty Dispatch,* February 20, 1969.

on a warning blow along the border. The most plausible interpretation of the ensuing clash is that Chinese troops first provoked and then ambushed and mauled a Soviet unit on the disputed island of Chenpao (or Damansky) on March 2.[36]

This clash precipitated a vigorous Soviet reaction, with Brezhnev and the "hawks" temporarily in ascendance once more—a reaction of which China was to be the victim but which had other aspects as well. The tension with Peking was used as a convenient rationalization for withdrawal from the Berlin "minicrisis." [37] This act of de-escalation in Berlin, as well as the fact that Moscow had been engaged since early 1968 in negotiations with Bonn, tended to degrade the effectiveness of the West German and Berlin issues as devices for rallying the Warsaw Pact states and enhancing Soviet influence over them. This tendency toward declining influence was an especially serious problem inasmuch as Moscow was in the process of renegotiating its bilateral alliances with the Warsaw Pact states and was doing its best to render the alliances operative against "any state or group of states," not merely an adversary in Europe. Moscow evidently found the Ussuri crisis and the apparent Chinese danger, which it exaggerated in its propaganda, a convenient device for rallying the Warsaw Pact states, promoting its objective of bringing the Mongolian People's Republic into the Warsaw Pact, and distracting East European attention insofar as possible from the failure of Soviet policy to prevent the extension of the NATO alliance (beyond April 1969). Such a failure could plausibly be attributed by Moscow's critics to the invasion of Czechoslovakia.

These devices at any rate were used by Brezhnev, with little success, to exploit the Ussuri fighting at a Warsaw Pact meeting held in Budapest on March 17, 1969.[38] Another area in which Moscow tried to gain political advantage from the Ussuri clash was India; Soviet Defense Minister Marshal Grechko arrived there on March 2, 1969, and before leaving he reportedly held talks with Indian officials on the coordination of policy toward China.[39] Moscow also took care to communicate its version of the Ussuri fighting and its views on the China question to

---

[36] Robinson, *op. cit.*, pp. 33-38.

[37] Paul Wohl, *Peking Expects Soviet Attack in October,* Investment Research, Equity Research Associates, New York, August 1969, p. 6.

[38] *Ibid.,* pp. 6, 8.

[39] Chinese resentment at the Grechko visit was expressed in a New China News Agency dispatch, March 11, 1969.

several non-Communist governments, including the United States and West Germany.[40]

Moscow was encouraged no doubt by the fact that Peking had seemingly eliminated any chance of American support—the possibility of a Sino-American rapprochement has been of acute Soviet concern since about 1966—by canceling on February 19, 1969, the Sino-American ambassadorial talks in Warsaw scheduled for February 20; and it reacted to the Ussuri clash in ways that evidently went beyond what Peking had anticipated, thereby causing alarm. In addition to diplomatic protests,[41] Moscow unleashed a massive anti-Chinese propaganda campaign, with particular emphasis on the heroic conduct of the outnumbered and surprised Soviet border guards and the inhuman behavior of the Chinese toward Russian dead and wounded.[42] On March 7, a highly organized "mob" demonstrated "spontaneously" against the Chinese embassy in Moscow and inflicted some damage.[43]

Soviet military calculations at that time may have been based not only on a natural desire to avenge the March 2 fight and teach Peking a lesson, but on a recollection of earlier Chinese behavior. Twice before, in October 1950 and September 1962, when Peking had felt threatened by American and Indian military advances, respectively, Chinese forces had struck initial warning blows, followed by later, much heavier, blows after the adversary had failed to heed the warning. Moscow, therefore, may have anticipated a second Chinese initiative in the Ussuri sector, especially in view of the massive anti-Soviet propaganda campaign that Peking had been mounting since March 2.[44] Certainly Soviet behavior indicated a determination on Moscow's part that the second blow should be struck from its side and not from Peking's. Political effect on the forthcoming Chinese Ninth Party Congress and the Warsaw Pact meeting in Budapest was probably hoped for.

On March 15, accordingly, a second, much fiercer, engagement was fought on Chenpao/Damansky. In spite of Soviet allegations of Chinese initiative—to be expected in any case—there is little doubt that this time it was the Soviet side that launched a devastating attack with superior

---

[40] Wohl, *Peking Expects . . .*, p. 6.

[41] Moscow and Peking exchanged notes on the clash on March 2.

[42] Cf. Associated Press dispatch from Moscow in *Washington Post,* March 8, 1969.

[43] Henry Kamm in *New York Times,* March 8, 1969.

[44] Cf. "Down with the New Tsars!" *People's Daily* and *Liberation Army Daily,* March 4, 1969.

firepower and heavy Chinese casualties.[45] Peking's alarm is indicated by the fact that it shortly began to reduce its propaganda exploitation of the border crisis.[46] Since the Ninth Party Congress actually opened on April 1, there is an obvious possibility that if it had been scheduled at one time for mid-March it was postponed on account of the second Ussuri clash.

In the meantime, Soviet policy seemed to reflect a rapid shift in favor of the "doves," led by Kosygin, at the expense of the "hawks," led by Brezhnev. On March 21, Kosygin tried to telephone Peking to discuss means of easing the border crisis. Probably after a debate in which Peking concluded that the lessening threat in Moscow justified a policy that was bold without being provocative, Peking replied in writing on March 22 that diplomatic channels rather than the telephone should be used.[47] It is highly probable that Kosygin and other Soviet moderates would be opposed to the idea of war with China on account of the serious damage it could do to the Soviet Union's political, economic, military, and international position. The question remains why this opposition to war seemed to gain the ascendancy so soon after the second Ussuri clash. The most plausible answer seems to be that four developments occurred at that time which, without adding much to the substance of the moderates' position, nevertheless provided them with useful arguments for winning over waverers in the Politburo. The first was the falling off of Chinese propaganda exploitation of the crisis, a possible indication of concern and an indication of lack of intent to stage another attack. The second was the fact that the effort to exploit the Chinese issue at the Warsaw Pact meeting had been unsuccessful. The third was that the Sino-Soviet border clashes were arousing acute anxiety in the minds of important foreign Communist leaders—an especially undesirable development since an international conference of Communist parties was forthcoming in June after being once postponed on account of the invasion of Czechoslovakia.[48] The fourth was that it could be alleged by Soviet moderates—not necessarily out of conviction but for effect on less sophisticated colleagues—that pressures on Peking

---

[45] Robinson, *op. cit.*, pp. 38-40.

[46] Cf. Stanley Karnow in *Washington Post,* March 22, 1969.

[47] Lin Piao's report to the Ninth Party Congress, April 1, 1969 (text released by New China News Agency, April 27, 1969).

[48] See, e.g., statement by Sanzo Nosaka, "The Chinese and Soviet Governments Should Settle the Border Dispute Through Talks," *Akahata,* March 18, 1969.

were threatening to "drive it into the arms" of the United States; U.S. Senator Edward M. Kennedy, in an important and widely publicized speech on March 20, speculated that Soviet behavior might be causing Peking to reappraise its attitude toward the United States and added that the latter should seize the opportunity to improve its relations with Peking.[49]

## Moscow's Deployment of Carrot and Stick

To the Soviet stick, which from the first Ussuri clash to the Kosygin telephone call was used exclusively, was now juxtaposed a carrot, in the form of a statement issued on March 29. After rehearsing Moscow's version of the March 2 and March 15 incidents, the statement further rehearsed the history of the Sino-Russian border, denied that the treaties were "unequal," affirmed the historic and recent Soviet friendship for China, summarized the growth of border tension since the early 1960s, warned Peking against further resort to force, and proposed the resumption of the 1964 border "consultations" as soon as possible.[50] On April 11, in a diplomatic note, Moscow proposed that the 1964 consultations be resumed in Moscow on April 15 (a date that had no chance of acceptance in view of the shortness of the time and the fact that Peking was then in the midst of holding its Ninth Party Congress), "or another time in the near future convenient to the Chinese side." [51]

The Soviet line was now sufficiently pacific to permit Peking to maintain the political position it had staked out in 1964. Lin Piao's report to the Ninth Party Congress, which was delivered on April 1 but not adopted until April 14 and not published until April 27, denounced the Soviet Union for its "revisionism," its invasion of Czechoslovakia, its proclamation of the Brezhnev Doctrine of "limited sovereignty," its insistence on the Sino-Soviet frontier as established by the "unequal" treaties, and its alleged recent aggression against China. While insisting that China would resist any Soviet attack, Lin Piao conceded that as in 1964 Peking agreed that the "unequal" treaties should be "taken as the basis for the settlement of the boundary question." The only possible inference from this statement was the immensely important one that

---

[49] This passage from the speech may be found in A. Doak Barnett and Edwin O. Reischauer, eds., *The United States and China: The Next Decade,* New York: Frederick A. Praeger, 1970, p. 155.

[50] Text broadcast by Tass, same date.

[51] Text broadcast by Radio Moscow, April 11, 1969.

Peking, fully aware of the possibly suicidal consequences of doing the opposite, was admitting that it had no serious intention of reclaiming any significant portion of the territories lost under the "unequal" treaties. On the other hand, Lin insisted that the Soviet Union had "occupied or attempted to occupy" certain unspecified Chinese territory "in violation of the treaties" and seemed to imply that this would have to be restored. As for the Soviet statement of March 29, Lin said merely that "Our government is considering its reply to this." [52]

The Chinese reply was forthcoming on May 24. It insisted that Peking's position on the current crisis was one of avoiding conflict, maintaining the status quo, and seeking negotiations (not merely "consultations" as demanded by Moscow). But it also insisted that Chenpao/Damansky was Chinese territory, even under the "unequal" treaties, and that the Soviet side had initiated both of the recent clashes on the island. The statement reiterated the Chinese position that the treaties were "unequal" and therefore implicitly invalid, that the Soviet Union in Lenin's day had agreed to review them, that the Soviet Union had occupied or at least claimed territory in the Pamir and Amur-Ussuri areas in excess of what had been gained under the treaties, and that Soviet initiatives had been entirely responsible for the tension along the frontier since about 1960. General Soviet foreign policy was denounced as aggressive and compared unfavorably with China's allegedly peaceful policy. Serious doubt was expressed as to Moscow's sincerity in calling for talks on the border issue. It was conceded once again that the treaties, even though emphatically "unequal," could be used as the basis for the renegotiated boundary. Each side in principle must return any territory it had occupied in violation of the treaties. The Soviet note of April 11 was rejected as unreasonable, and it was proposed instead that "the date and place for the Sino-Soviet boundary negotiations be discussed and decided upon by both sides through diplomatic channels." On the other hand, the Chinese side would certainly defend itself if attacked again.[53]

Moscow's reply, dated June 13, was somewhat harsher in tone than the statement of March 29. It demanded the resumption of the 1964 "consultations" in Moscow within two to three months and added, almost as an ultimatum, that "The Soviet government expects the CPR government to inform it shortly whether the above proposals on the dates and

---

[52] See note 47.

[53] See note 33.

place for the continuation of the consultations are acceptable to it." [54]

In the meantime, on June 7, Brezhnev, trying with little success at the international conference of Communist parties to exploit the Chinese issue to Soviet advantage, had included a denunciation of Peking in his speech to the conference. He also made his well known but rather cryptic suggestion of a "system of collective security in Asia." [55] In response to Chinese charges that Moscow was trying to rig up a "new anti-China military bloc," [56] subsequent Soviet statements insisted that China was welcome to join the "system." [57] Soviet Foreign Minister Andrei Gromyko's remarks on China in his speech to the Supreme Soviet on July 10, however, were lengthy and stern and included a reminder that Moscow insisted on Peking's resuming the 1964 "consultations" shortly.[58]

Of much greater concern to Peking than Moscow's statements was the massive buildup of Soviet forces, including powerful offensive units presumably equipped with tactical nuclear weapons.[59] About the beginning of August a new commander, Colonel General V. F. Tolubko, was appointed for the Soviet Far Eastern Military District. Compounding the menace implicit in the fact that Tolubko was a general of the missile forces,[60] he was the author of an article published in *Red Star* commemorating the outbreak of the only Sino-Soviet war to date (in 1929). After "all efforts to settle the conflict by peaceful means had failed," he wrote, the Soviet forces struck a "sudden and decisive blow." [61] This was by no means the only threat of Soviet military action against China made during the summer of 1969. Late in August Western analysts became aware that Moscow had been querying European Communist leaders as to their reactions to a Soviet attack, either an invasion or a "surgical

---

[54] Soviet statement of June 13, 1969 (text released by Tass, same date).

[55] Brezhnev speech published in *Pravda,* June 8, 1969.

[56] New China News Agency statement, June 28, 1969; Chou En-lai speech released by New China News Agency, July 13, 1969.

[57] See, e.g., broadcast by Vladimir Volokholansky, Radio Moscow, July 8, 1969.

[58] Text in *Pravda,* July 11, 1969.

[59] Cf. Harrison E. Salisbury in *New York Times,* May 7 and May 24, 1969. The buildup was denounced in a broadcast by Peking Domestic Service on August 14, 1969. For a professional appraisal of the military situation see "The Military Balance Between the Soviet Union and China," *The Military Balance 1970-1971,* London: Institute for Strategic Studies, 1970, pp. 99-101.

[60] CZ, "New Red Army Commander for Chinese Border," Radio Free Europe Research Paper, August 8, 1968.

[61] V. F. Tolubko, "The Glory of Heroes Lives," *Red Star,* August 6, 1969.

strike," against the Chinese nuclear installations.[62] A *Pravda* editorial of August 28 denounced Peking for its general behavior and for its failure to reply to the Soviet statement of June 13. It added that "War, should it break out under present conditions and with present day devices, because of the lethal weapons and the present means of their delivery would not leave a single continent unaffected." [63]

During this period each adversary was busily trying, by radio broadcasts, to incite disaffection among the minority peoples of the other's border region.[64]

The Soviet military buildup and threats were accompanied by a series of usually small-scale clashes along the Amur River and at the western end of Sinkiang.[65] The initiative generally appears to have been Soviet, at least in the most important of these—an engagement occurring in western Sinkiang on August 13, the first of the alternative deadlines set by the Soviet statement of June 13.

In effect, Peking was being given to understand that the alternative to "consultations" was war.

---

[62] Cf. Chalmers Roberts in *Washington Post,* August 28, 1969; Hedrick Smith in *New York Times,* August 29, 1969; Anthony Astrachan in *Washington Post,* August 29, 1969.

[63] "The Adventurist Course of Peking," *Pravda,* August 28, 1969.

[64] John Gittings, "Guessing with Guns," *Far Eastern Economic Review,* August 21, 1969, p. 443.

[65] Chinese notes of protest sent June 6, June 11, July 8, August 13, August 19, 1969 (texts released by New China News Agency on those dates). Soviet notes of protest sent June 11, July 8, August 13, 1969 (texts released by Tass on those dates).

# 2
# Peking's Diplomatic Management of the Crisis

Until November 1968 Peking, although perturbed by the invasion of Czechoslovakia and the Brezhnev Doctrine, claimed to see no reason why either those developments or the effects of the Cultural Revolution on China's foreign relations required major steps to improve China's diplomatic position and thereby gain political support against a possible Soviet threat. The official Maoist line was that no such necessity existed. In the words of the communique of the Twelfth Plenary Session of the Party Central Committee, issued on October 31, "We are not in the least isolated, for the people who want revolution, comprising over 90 percent of the world's population, are our friends." [1]

## The Trend Toward Diplomatic Normalization

The Chinese leadership was certainly too sophisticated, however, to believe that the "people who want revolution" were capable of being of much immediate help to Peking against current Soviet pressures. The most effective source of such help, if it could be obtained, would be the United States; it was undoubtedly remembered in Peking that President Johnson had spoken out on behalf of Romania at the end of August 1968, and that his statement had seemed to contribute to calming Soviet-Romanian tension. The obstacles to approaching the United States for support—let alone obtaining it—were obvious: Maoist ideological hostility to American "imperialism," and Sino-American conflicts of interest in Asia (notably over Taiwan, Indochina, and Japan). But the more pressing reality was the Soviet threat; Mao, in his unpublished speech to

---

[1] Text released by New China News Agency, November 1, 1968.

the Twelfth Plenary Session, is believed to have said that the Soviet Union was the greater enemy and that Peking must seek an improvement in its relations with the West, apparently including the United States.[2]

During November the seriousness of the obstacles to such an approach, at least as compared with the undesirability of isolation in the face of possible Soviet pressures, seemed from Peking's view to diminish somewhat. Early in the month, the United States ceased the regular bombing of North Vietnam that had been in progress since February 1965, and the Paris talks on Vietnam, which the United States and North Vietnam had begun the previous May, began to show greater promise as a result of the inclusion of representatives of the Saigon government and the National Liberation Front. The outcome of the American election also appeared promising, since the winner, Richard M. Nixon, had the reputation of being strongly anti-Soviet and had spoken during the campaign of "building bridges" to China. It appears likely that shortly afterward, perhaps about the end of November, Mao Tse-tung went on vacation or became ill, and was not actively in charge in Peking until the second half of January 1969.[3] Whether or not he gave consent before going away to a gesture toward the United States, his absence probably had the effect of making such a move easier for Chou En-lai, who had the effective management of China's foreign relations.

On November 24, the New China News Agency broadcast the text of a report that Mao had made on March 4, 1949.[4] The extensive publicity on the report stressed entirely its domestic content,[5] perhaps to distract the attention of the general public from more esoteric matters. The report includes, however, the statement that "We are preparing to have negotiations with the reactionary Nanking government" [6]—which in fact failed in April 1949 on account of Communist inflexibility. This failure, plus the nature of Mao's "latest instruction" announced on November 24 ("Historical experience merits attention"), suggests that a message was being conveyed to the initiated to the effect that flexibility

[2] Stanley Karnow in *Washington Post,* February 20, 1969.

[3] Cf. John Gittings, "Peking Walls Have Ears Too," *Far Eastern Economic Review,* January 30, 1969, pp. 175-176.

[4] "Report to the Second Plenary Session of the Seventh Central Committee of the Communist Party of China," March 5, 1949, *Selected Works of Mao Tse-tung,* vol. iv, Peking: Foreign Languages Press, 1961, pp. 361-374.

[5] Especially "Study the History of the Struggle Between the Two Lines Conscientiously," *People's Daily, Red Flag,* and *Liberation Army Daily,* November 25, 1968.

[6] *Selected Works of Mao Tse-tung,* vol. iv, p. 371.

was a proven necessity and that considerations of flexibility indicated it was again time to try negotiating with an adversary.

On November 25, 1968, an invitation was sent from the Chinese embassy in Warsaw to the American ambassador there proposing that a session of the Sino-American ambassadorial talks—suspended since January 8, 1968—be held on February 20, 1969, a month after President Nixon's inauguration. The next day a foreign ministry spokesman in Peking, commenting on the invitation, denounced the United States in Maoist language (necessary if only for internal consumption) for obstructing the talks, and in particular for having refused to accept two demands that Peking had made "consistently" during the talks. One was that the United States withdraw all its "armed forces" from Taiwan and the Taiwan Strait; the other was that the two sides "conclude an agreement on the Five Principles of Peaceful Coexistence." [7] This appears to have been the first time that Peking had called publicly for an agreement with the United States embodying the Five Principles of Peaceful Coexistence, as distinct from calling for Sino-American relations to be conducted "in accordance with" those principles.[8]

Informed sources in Japan believed that the period of preparation for the resumption of the Warsaw talks was also intended in Peking to witness a major move toward normalization of China's external relations after the Cultural Revolution, through the return of Peking's ambassadors to their posts; all but one of these ambassadors (to the United Arab Republic) had been withdrawn in 1967.[9]

But contrary to Japanese opinion, the outcome was quite different: No ambassadors were returned to their posts, and no talks were held with the United States. The reason is almost certainly Mao Tse-tung's return to active life about the middle of January 1969; he was in one of his militant moods reinforced no doubt by discussions during his absence with his extremist advisers, such as his wife Chiang Ching. The first overt sign both of his return and of his mood was his appearance at a rally on January 25, which was attended by some 40,000 "revolutionary fighters" of the People's Liberation Army, as well as by virtually the whole Chinese Communist leadership. The press release on the rally, which was very militant in tone, stressed that it was essential for the Chinese public to

---

[7] Text released by New China News Agency, November 26, 1968.

[8] Cf. Bernard Gwertzman in *New York Times,* November 27, 1968.

[9] David K. Willis in *Christian Science Monitor,* February 20, 1969.

"closely follow Chairman Mao's great strategic plan" and to promote "preparedness against war." [10] Another news release asserted that the Chinese people and armed forces were determined to "greet the forthcoming Ninth National Congress of the Party with concrete action." [11] It is quite possible that Mao's "great strategic plan" included the promotion of a campaign of "war preparations" and perhaps some anti-Soviet border incidents which would create a militant climate congenial to the Maoists for the Ninth Party Congress; in any event, it is not difficult to see why Moscow might have been alarmed and angered by the tone of Peking's pronouncements.

It is fairly easy to construct a plausible rationale for Mao's ruling out of diplomatic normalization, and especially the talks with the United States, at that time. He evidently did not take the Soviet threat seriously and therefore saw no reason to appease the United States. On the contrary, he apparently considered the time ripe, especially in view of the approach of the Party Congress, to reaffirm the dual adversary strategy of simultaneous political struggle against the United States and the Soviet Union, which he had followed since about 1960. The idea of a formal agreement with American "imperialism" on any major political subject, including the Five Principles of Peaceful Coexistence, is questionable by Maoist standards, if only because the United States is alleged to be uncooperative and untrustworthy.[12] President Nixon could be portrayed plausibly, in Maoist eyes, as fitting this description and Peking, after a relatively mild commentary (January 22) on Nixon's inaugural address, published a much stronger one on January 27.[13] A statement by President Nixon at a press conference the same day, to the effect that the United States would continue to oppose Peking's admission to the United Nations,[14] may have discouraged those in Peking who wanted to go ahead with the talks. Given the preoccupation of the Chinese leadership with preparations for the Ninth Party Congress and

---

[10] New China News Agency dispatch, January 25, 1969.

[11] New China News Agency dispatch, January 27, 1969.

[12] Cf. ". . . intrinsically the imperialists are unwilling to accept the Five Principles of Peaceful Coexistence" ("Peaceful Coexistence—Two Diametrically Opposed Policies," *People's Daily* and *Red Flag*, December 12, 1963).

[13] "Confession in an Impasse—a Comment on Nixon's Inaugural Address and the Despicable Applause by the Soviet Revisionist Renegade Clique," *People's Daily* and *Red Flag*, January 27, 1969.

[14] Text in *Major Public Statements on China by U.S. Officials (1969-1970)*, U.S. Information Agency, January 1971, pp. 1-2.

with nondiplomatic ways of coping with the Soviet Union, there was little likelihood of being able to send an ambassador to Warsaw or anywhere else by February 20, 1969. The last straw to continuing the talks was the defection from the Chinese embassy in The Hague on January 24 of Liao Ho-shu, of the Chinese embassy, who later took refuge in the American Embassy.[15] Peking unsuccessfully demanded his return on February 6 [16] and then on February 18 cited Liao's case as the basis for canceling the talks; nothing was said about the possibility of talks at some later date.[17] During the next few weeks, Maoism reigned supreme in Peking's public comments on the United States as the Chinese press repeatedly hailed the activities of "progressive" American students.[18]

Even the Sino-Soviet clashes on the Ussuri did not produce a change in Peking's public attitude toward the United States or a beginning of general diplomatic normalization. But when the congress (April 1-24, 1969) was over and the Soviet menace was preoccupying Peking's attention, the Chinese leadership at least refrained from denouncing, as it would have done in the past, the various American gestures toward it that began in mid-1969. Peking, however, did not go so far as to welcome those gestures, which comprised private overtures for a resumption of the ambassadorial talks at Warsaw, a limited relaxation of restrictions on trade with and travel to mainland China by American citizens, and the announcement of the Nixon Doctrine, with its strong overtones of American military withdrawal from the Far East and the Western Pacific. Indeed, some Chinese interest was expressed, in conversations with nationals of third countries, in trade and other forms of Sino-American contact. There were apparently well founded reports that Peking was considering inviting a limited number of carefully selected American visitors. This trend, limited as it was, probably reflected a belief in the utility of some "bridges" to the United States as a form of restraint on the Soviet Union. Another probable factor was the growing influence, on account of the Sino-Soviet border crisis and the end of the Cultural Revolution, of the relatively moderate Chou En-lai; he, how-

---

[15] Cf. the careful analysis by Guy Searls in *Christian Science Monitor,* February 25, 1969.

[16] New China News Agency dispatch, February 6, 1969.

[17] Foreign Ministry statement released by New China News Agency, February 18, 1969.

[18] Cf. *Christian Science Monitor,* March 17, 1969.

ever, in view of his experience of February 1969 did not go so far as to show interest in a resumption of the ambassadorial talks at Warsaw.

The Nixon Doctrine was probably received in Peking with mixed feelings; it seemed to foreshadow a reduction of the American military threat to China and perhaps of American support for Taiwan, but possibly also United States unwillingness to act as a counterweight in Asia to the Soviet Union and Japan. There is little doubt that at that time Peking wanted at least a declaration of support from the United States such as had been made on behalf of Romania a year earlier. What it received instead was a statement by U.S. Under Secretary of State Elliot L. Richardson on September 5 deploring the tension between the Soviet Union and China and declining to take sides.[19] No doubt the United States government had been impressed with the Soviet warning implicit in a *Pravda* editorial of August 28 to "keep hands off the Sino-Soviet crisis." [20]

On September 11, the same day on which Chou was to talk with Kosygin about the reduction of tension, he talked with Romanian Premier Maurer.[21] It seems possible that Chou asked Maurer whether President Nixon, when visiting Bucharest at the beginning of August, had indicated any intention of supporting China, as President Johnson had supported Romania, and if such was the case, that Maurer replied in the negative.

It proved much easier for Peking to normalize its diplomatic relations with countries with which they already existed; this was done in the hope of gaining support against the Soviet Union. Peking was undoubtedly perturbed by Moscow's utilization of its superior diplomatic facilities, at the time of the Ussuri clashes, for explaining its case to and soliciting understanding from key foreign governments. Furthermore, the end of the Cultural Revolution clearly rendered appropriate the termination sooner or later of the diplomatic anomalies to which it had given rise, and the Ussuri clashes provided an effective and convenient incentive for beginning to do so.

The normalization of Peking's general diplomatic posture had finally to wait until after the Ninth Party Congress, which took precedence over practically every other consideration. Normalization actually began on April 25, 1969, the day after the closing of the congress, when elderly

---

[19] Text in *Major Public Statements. . .*, p. 22.
[20] Cf. *New York Times,* October 9, 1969.
[21] New China News Agency dispatch, September 11, 1969.

Vice Chairman Tung Pi-wu emerged from the obscurity that had shrouded him during the Cultural Revolution and began to function as acting chief of state to the extent of accepting the credentials of newly arrived foreign ambassadors.[22] Four days later, the day after the adjournment of the First Plenary Session of the new party Central Committee elected at the Ninth Congress, Chou En-lai began to receive a series of foreign ambassadors,[23] and on May Day he joined Mao, Lin Piao, and a fourth Politburo Standing Committee member, K'ang Sheng, in greeting several ambassadors from friendly foreign countries on the rostrum in Tienanmen Square.[24]

Beginning in mid-May, Peking commenced filling vacant ambassadorships in countries with which diplomatic relations already existed and which were considered to be friendly or especially important. In each case where there was no ambassador from that country in China at the time, Peking insisted as a matter of "face" on receiving one before sending an ambassador in return. The first country to which Peking sent an ambassador—one considered to be of special political and symbolic importance—was Albania. The second was France, which was probably selected for its value as a listening post and contact point but also because it is a permanent member of the United Nations Security Council—a fact that might be highly significant if Sino-Soviet tension should turn into a "threat to the peace" within the meaning of the United Nations Charter. On these two key countries were bestowed the only two ambassadors to have been elected to the Central Committee at the Ninth Party Congress. Keng Piao, who went to Tirana, Albania, is a person of such importance that when he was recalled at the end of 1970 it was to give him the post of Director of the International Liaison Department of the Central Committee, a body that deals with foreign Communist parties. Huang Chen, who went to Paris, was the only ambassador who returned to the post he had occupied before 1967.[25] By mid-July 1969, seventeen ambassadors had been sent to friendly Afro-Asian and European countries.[26] Then, probably because of Peking's preoccupation with the Sino-

---

[22] New China News Agency dispatch, April 25, 1969.

[23] New China News Agency dispatch, April 29, 1969.

[24] New China News Agency dispatch, May 1, 1969.

[25] Cf. Guy Searls in *Christian Science Monitor,* May 27, 1969.

[26] Albania, France, North Vietnam, Cambodia, Pakistan, Tanzania, Zambia, Guinea, Algeria, and Yemen, in that order. South Yemen received a chargé d'affaires.

Soviet crisis and the beginning of the Sino-Soviet negotiations, no more were sent until March 1970, when another series began with North Korea, and continued into 1971. Ambassadors have been sent by now to all the Communist states, even the Soviet Union and Yugoslavia, with one exception—Mongolia, probably because that country is considered to be under Soviet military occupation and to be an accessory to Soviet pressures on China.

These countries, all friendly from Peking's point of view, had been voting for Peking in the United Nations (i.e., against the "important question" resolution and for the Albanian resolution; see Chapter 5). The period of Sino-Soviet tension following the Ninth Party Congress probably contributed to an increased interest on Peking's part in entering the United Nations. This interest, although generally accepted, is not easy to document. To be sure, the tone of Peking's editorial comment on its defeat in the 1969 United Nations vote [27] was slightly less bitter than that on the same occasion the year before.[28] The main evidence for the increase in interest in joining the UN was in the form of private conversations between Chinese officials and foreign diplomats or other visitors.[29]

An important aspect of China's diplomatic normalization campaign has been Canada's diplomatic recognition of Peking in October 1969 and the subsequent recognitions for which it served as the entering wedge. The fact that Peking, at Ottawa's request, agreed as early as the beginning of February 1969 to open talks with the Canadian government in Stockholm shows that the Ussuri clashes cannot have provided the original motivation for the talks. The fact that from the beginning Peking laid heavy emphasis on Canadian recognition of Peking's claim to Taiwan,[30] however, is suggestive. During the previous year, Moscow had inaugurated an intensive program of informal contacts with Nationalist Chinese officials and citizens, presumably for the main purpose of convincing Peking, through psychological and political pressure, that Moscow was contemplating the adoption of a "two Chinas" policy, but also to discourage Peking from responding to the overtures being made by the United

---

[27] ". . . the United Nations has all along been manipulated by U.S. imperialism" (New China News Agency dispatch, November 16, 1969).

[28] The United Nations "is nothing but U.S. imperialism's tool for aggression" (New China News Agency dispatch, November 21, 1968).

[29] Cf. Sam Pope Brewer in *New York Times,* September 18, 1969.

[30] Jay Walz in *New York Times,* February 10, 1969.

States. The most spectacular of these contacts was a visit to Taiwan in October 1968 [31] by Victor Louis, a Soviet journalist often used for sensitive quasi-diplomatic missions.[32] This visit may have contributed to the emphasis laid on the Taiwan question in the Chinese negotiations with Canada. If so, the fact that in the statement finally worked out between Peking and Ottawa in October 1970 the Chinese accepted a mere statement by the Canadians that Canada "took note" of Peking's claim to Taiwan may be related to the decrease in Soviet contacts with the Nationalist Chinese since about the beginning of the Peking talks in October 1969.

Some important observations can be made about Peking's campaign of diplomatic normalization—a campaign which has been highly successful especially in the United Nations, and which has included the strengthening of ties with the two key neighboring states of North Korea and North Vietnam. One is that Peking has not moderated its foreign policy to the extent of dropping support for "people's wars," as it very nearly did in the mid-1950s. Another is that the degree to which Peking has tried to exploit its improved diplomatic posture directly for anti-Soviet purposes has been limited. Peking undoubtedly remembers that its anti-Soviet maneuvers contributed largely to the wrecking of the scheduled Afro-Asian Conference of 1965, and also that the Soviet Union is still too influential in many places for Peking to gain much by attacking it overtly when not under obvious Soviet pressure. Indeed, Peking has not been under such pressure since October 1969. A third observation is that beginning with the partial easing of Sino-Soviet tension about that time, the signing of the Nixon-Sato (Japanese Prime Minister Eisaku Sato) declaration in November 1969 and the Cambodian crisis resulting from the overthrow of Prince Sihanouk in the spring of 1970, and for about a year thereafter, Peking saw more advantage in concentrating its propaganda, in Asia in particular, against the United States and Japan, rather than against the Soviet Union.

**Coping with Moscow**

Peking's diplomatic management of the Soviet threat was mainly in the competent hands of Chou En-lai. Chou, however, had at the same time to ensure himself against a recrudescence of Maoist pressures of the kind

---

[31] Cf. Stanley Karnow in *Washington Post,* February 17, 1969.

[32] See the exchange of letters between Louis and Abraham Brumberg in *Problems of Communism,* vol. xviii, no. 6 (November-December 1969), pp. 68-69.

that had wrecked the Sino-American ambassadorial talks scheduled for February 20, 1969. Even before issuing his reply of May 24 (see Chapter 1) to the Soviet statement of March 29, Chou had begun to engage Moscow in diplomatic dialogue. On May 11, the chairman of the Chinese delegation accepted, in rather hostile language, a Soviet proposal of April 26 for a reconvening of the Sino-Soviet commission on border river navigation.[33] After convening at Khabarovsk (referred to by the Chinese as Poli) on June 18, and despite some difficulties, the commission concluded its usual unpublished agreement in early August.[34]

These specialized talks, however, were far from satisfying the Soviet demand for "consultations" on the border question. Whatever Chou En-lai's real attitude toward these "consultations," he did not agree to them until Peking had been subjected to further military, psychological, and diplomatic pressures.

On September 3, 1969, the day before his regime's National Day, North Vietnamese Chairman Ho Chi Minh died. The following day Chou En-lai arrived in Hanoi to pay his last respects.[35] He left a day later, without waiting for the funeral, probably because, from the beginning of the Cultural Revolution, Peking had regarded as politically questionable the going abroad of a top leader, and also because the crisis with Moscow required his presence in Peking.[36] But his visit had almost certainly been long enough to enable him to assess Hanoi's attitude toward the Sino-Soviet crisis. With very little risk of error this attitude may be reconstructed as one of great apprehension combined with a keen desire for Sino-Soviet talks on easing the tension. The reasons for the apprehension are fairly obvious. A major Sino-Soviet crisis would force Hanoi to declare for one side or the other, a choice it has always avoided; if it were forced to do so, it would have little choice but to declare for China: this step in turn might lead to an undesirable increase of Chinese influence and to Soviet reprisals. Second, the crisis seemed to threaten the routes for Soviet military equipment moving across China to North Vietnam; this equipment was not as necessary as it had been before the cessation of American bombing of North Vietnam, but its unhampered arrival was still highly desirable.

---

33 New China News Agency dispatch, May 12, 1969.

34 New China News Agency dispatch, August 11, 1969.

35 Peking Domestic Service broadcast, September 4, 1969.

36 Another possibility is that Mao suffered a medical crisis at that time. Rumors to this effect were spread, and Moscow denied Chinese charges of having circulated them.

Chou was sufficiently impressed by Hanoi's position to send his most trusted civilian collaborator, Vice Premier Li Hsien-nien, as the head of the Chinese delegation to Ho's funeral. Hanoi no doubt pressed on Li and on Kosygin, who attended the funeral on Moscow's behalf, the urgent desirability of talks. There is reason to believe that Moscow would have welcomed immediate talks in Hanoi. According to information later given to the Japanese Communist leader Sanzo Nosaka in Hanoi, however, Kosygin also proposed that on his way home he hold talks with Chou in Peking. By the time Kosygin was ready to leave Hanoi on September 10, however, Peking had not replied, and he therefore started for home. At Calcutta he received a message from Peking to the effect that he would be welcome, but at the airport only and without protocol. He evidently radioed Moscow for approval of these conditions and flew to Dushanbe, in Soviet Central Asia, where he received an affirmative reply. He thereupon altered course and arrived at Peking on September 11, where he talked for four hours at the airport with Chou En-lai.[37]

Neither side needed to be reminded that the three-month deadline for "consultations" on the border issue imposed in the Soviet statement of June 13 had nearly arrived. It is improbable that Kosygin uttered any threats, since a sufficient number had already been made. The Chinese announcement [38] described the talks as "frank"—an implication that there was a lack of agreement. According to seemingly reliable Soviet sources,[39] Kosygin proposed "normalization" of the border situation through "consultations" at the deputy foreign minister level, the reestablishment of the "hot line" between Moscow and Peking (presumably the same line that Kosygin had used on March 21), an exchange of ambassadors, an increase in trade, overflight rights for Soviet aircraft bound for North Vietnam, and ideological discussions to be conducted later under appropriate conditions (i.e., without public polemics). The Chinese version [40] is substantially in agreement with the Soviet and adds that the Chinese demanded that both sides withdraw from all disputed areas and

---

[37] Kyodo (Tokyo) dispatch, September 12, 1969. See also Christian Duevel, "Kosygin's Surprise Visit to Peking," *Radio Liberty Dispatch,* September 12, 1969.

[38] New China News Agency dispatch, September 11, 1969.

[39] As reported by Gus Hall (Harrison E. Salisbury in *New York Times,* September 25, 1969) and Istvan Körmendy (*Magyarorszag,* Budapest, August 2, 1970). On overflight rights see Bernard Gwertzman in *New York Times,* October 1, 1969.

[40] Chinese statement of October 7, 1969 (text released by New China News Agency, same date).

avoid further clashes. Presumably each man undertook to report the other's proposals to his colleagues.

During the following weeks, Peking gave evidence of the seriousness with which it regarded the military situation by avoiding frontier incidents.[41] Moscow for its part ceased its polemics against China,[42] and there is evidence that the troops of both sides withdrew somewhat from the frontier so as to break contact, without necessarily going so far as to evacuate the disputed areas.[43]

The main problem at this point evidently was the reluctance of Mao Tse-tung and the true believers among his colleagues to yield under pressure and to reach an agreement with Soviet "revisionism" (or "social-imperialism" as it had often been called in China since the Ussuri clashes). The first overt indication that this problem persisted was the militant Maoist tone of the slogans for the forthcoming National Day (October 1), which were published on September 16, 1969. The twenty-second of these read: [44]

> People of all countries, unite and oppose any war of aggression launched by imperialism or social-imperialism, especially a war of aggression in which atom bombs are used as weapons! The people of the world should use revolutionary war to eliminate the war of aggression, should such a war break out, and preparations must be made against it right now!

It must have appeared in Moscow that additional threats were needed to remind Mao of the precariousness of his position and to help Chou En-lai in coping with the Maoist resistance to concessions, or even to "consultations." That same evening (September 16, 1969), the London *Evening News* carried an extraordinary article by its Moscow correspondent Victor Louis, who reminded his readers that Moscow still possessed both the capability and the will to invade China or knock out its nuclear installations, or both. This threat was undoubtedly promptly relayed to Peking by its mission in London. On September 18, Peking sent a note to Moscow in which, according to the later Chinese account,[45] it reiterated its proposal for a ceasefire and a troop withdrawal. When no reply was received, Peking on October 6 [46] sent another note to the

---

41 Bernard Gwertzman in *New York Times,* September 19, 1969.

42 Bernard Gwertzman in *New York Times,* September 17, 1969.

43 Cf. Stanley Karnow in *Washington Post,* October 20, 1969.

44 New China News Agency dispatch, September 16, 1969.

45 See note 40.

46 *Ibid.*

same effect. It seems probable, however, that this time some Chinese concessions were made, because on October 7 Peking announced that agreement had just been reached to hold negotiations (not merely "consultations," as originally demanded by Moscow) at the deputy foreign minister level in Peking (not in Moscow as demanded by the Soviet Union). The date was said to be "under discussion." To show that Peking had no intention of entering into any ideological or other basic compromises, it was affirmed that "irreconcilable differences of principle" existed between the two sides.[47]

The following day, the Chinese Foreign Ministry (i.e., Chou En-lai), clearly in an effort to elucidate some of those differences and to establish that it was not giving way under Soviet pressure, although in fact it was, issued a lengthy "refutation" of the Soviet statement of June 13 [48] (see Chapter 1). The statement denounced the history of Russian and Soviet territorial expansion at the expense of China and other countries in Asia and Europe and reiterated the terms for a border settlement laid down in the statement of May 24.

To all outward indications, the two sides were as far apart as ever on the substance of the border dispute. Under considerable coercion, Peking had made only one demonstrable concession: it had stopped evading the Soviet demand for border talks. Moscow, for its part, made it clear as preparations for the talks got under way that it had no intention of compromising its ideological differences with Peking for the sake of an agreement on the border question and other matters pertaining to state relations.[49]

**The Peking Talks**

The talks began on October 20, 1969, between delegations led by Chinese Deputy Foreign Minister Ch'iao Kuan-hua and Soviet Deputy Foreign Minister V. V. Kuznetsov, who had served as Soviet ambassador to Peking immediately after Stalin's death. The progress of the talks remained almost totally secret, but it can be assumed that the differences of substance and priority were much the same as those that had been

---

[47] *Ibid.*

[48] Chinese statement of October 8, 1969 (text released by New China News Agency, same date).

[49] Cf. M. Suslov, "Leninism and the Revolutionary Transformation of the World," *Kommunist,* no. 15 (October 10, 1969), pp. 13-37.

expressed in the Chou-Kosygin talks. Each side probably hoped for a softening of the other's position, as a result of some policy shift.

It is known that the Soviet side, despite its obvious military superiority, suffered from political embarrassments beyond the basic considerations underlying its decision not to go to war with Peking. Moscow was careful to begin its talks with Peking a month before its representatives sat down at last with the United States for the Strategic Arms Limitation Talks (SALT), partly because it wished to avoid even the appearance of finding it easier to negotiate with "imperialism" than with a country which, for all its faults, was at least "socialist." Nor did Moscow want to give the impression that it was being pushed to the conference table with the United States by its difficulties with Peking. Accordingly, it began to circulate informally a misleading report that the talks in Peking were going well. The Chinese determination not to let Moscow succeed in this tactic was expressed in a similarly informal way, through a Communist-controlled but technically unofficial English language periodical published in Hong Kong.[50] An article appearing in that source early in November stated that "According to impressions gained recently by our correspondent in Peking, the Sino-Soviet negotiations on the boundary question have not been proceeding smoothly as some in the outside world have made them out to be." The article repeated that the Chinese position was that both sides should first reach agreement on "maintaining the status quo of the border, averting armed conflicts, and the disengagement of the armed forces of both sides from the disputed areas along the border." After that agreement, an "all-round settlement of the boundary question" would be possible, given sincerity on the Soviet side. But, the article concluded, "there is yet no sign of progress on the boundary negotiations, for all that our correspondent has been able to learn."

Peking, despite the facts that Soviet anti-Chinese polemics and contacts with the Nationalist Chinese were virtually suspended after the beginning of the talks, that border clashes had almost ceased, and that those which occurred were not being publicized, was seriously concerned over the state of its relations with the Soviet Union, even though it characteristically continued to issue propaganda blasts against Moscow. The SALT talks, like all major United States-Soviet negotiations, those on disarmament in particular, were interpreted in Peking as a case of

---

[50] "No Sign Yet of Progress in Sino-Soviet Border Talks," *Ta Kung Pao Weekly Supplement,* November 6-12, 1969.

"collusion" and "nuclear blackmail" against "the peoples of the world and against China in particular." [51] More urgently, Peking was concerned that the evident Soviet refusal to agree to a ceasefire and troop withdrawal from the border might indicate an intent to force a breakdown of the talks that would serve as a pretext for an attack.[52]

Chinese nervousness rose to a peak when Kuznetsov suspended the talks and returned with his military deputy, Major General V. A. Matrosov, to Moscow on December 14, ostensibly to take part in an approaching session of the Supreme Soviet but probably also to brief the leadership on the status of the talks and receive fresh instructions.[53] The possibility of breakdown of the talks was suggested by a resurgence in early December of published Soviet statements that appeared to threaten China with war.[54]

It was against this backdrop that Peking invoked the best of the available counterweights, the United States. Since early October, Peking had been telling diplomats of third countries that it was interested in resuming the Warsaw talks; and on December 3 the Chinese and American ambassadors to Poland held a conversation at a reception.[55] A more formal meeting on December 12 [56]—held to the accompaniment of anti-American editorials in the Chinese press—and another on January 8, 1970,[57] led to an agreement to resume the Sino-American ambassadorial talks on January 20. Another session of the talks was held on February 20. This period, like that in late 1968 when a resumption of the talks had been in preparation, corresponded with one of Mao Tse-tung's periodic prolonged absences from public view.[58] On April 27, to the accompaniment of anti-American editorials but in spite of the tension over Cambodia, Peking announced that another session of the talks would be held, on May 20.[59] In May, following the entry of American troops into Cambodia, Mao reappeared; and on May 20—the day that had been set for the next session of the Warsaw talks, but

[51] See, e.g. New China News Agency statement, November 4, 1969.
[52] Cf. Stanley Karnow in *Washington Post*, November 7 and 21, 1969; Paul Wohl in *Christian Science Monitor*, November 21, 1969.
[53] Cf. Paul Wohl in *Christian Science Monitor*, January 7, 1970.
[54] Paul Wohl in *Christian Science Monitor*, December 26, 1969.
[55] Peter Grose in *New York Times*, December 5, 1969.
[56] Clyde H. Farnsworth in *New York Times*, December 13, 1969.
[57] New China News Agency dispatch, January 9, 1970.
[58] Tad Szulc in *New York Times*, March 8, 1970.
[59] New China News Agency dispatch, April 27, 1970.

which Peking had canceled on May 18 [60]—Mao issued a statement denouncing the United States for its intervention in Cambodia.[61] Mao's negative attitude toward talks with the Soviet "social imperialists," as well as with the American "imperialists," no doubt partially explains his indifference to the usefulness of contacts with the United States as a means of coping with Moscow; it is significant, however, that this time the Chinese statement breaking off the Warsaw talks—unlike the similar statement of February 1969 issued before the Ussuri clashes—indicated an interest in resuming the talks at some future time and under more favorable circumstances. Mao and his colleagues were also undoubtedly convinced that Moscow did not intend to break off the Peking talks: Soviet propaganda reaction to the resumption of the Sino-American ambassadorial talks concentrated its attacks on Washington, not on Peking.[62]

Kuznetsov had returned to Peking on January 2, 1970 [63] and the talks were evidently resumed on January 5.[64] In spite of the abundant evidence of dissatisfaction on both sides with the way in which the talks were going,[65] it is clear in retrospect that, despite occasional rumblings from Soviet hawks,[66] the arguments in Moscow against war with China held the ascendancy over those in favor of war.[67] One indication of this was that the massive Soviet Army "Dvina" maneuvers of early 1970 were held in Byelorussia, almost as far as possible from the Chinese frontier; indeed, their location suggests that Moscow's anti-Chinese obsession of 1969 was giving way to a more normal priority for East and Central European affairs. In keeping with this mood, Kuznetsov seems to have returned to Peking with instructions to discuss in a flexible spirit [68] specific Chinese territorial claims in the Amu-Ussuri

[60] New China News Agency dispatch, May 19, 1970.
[61] Mao Tse-tung, "People of the World, Unite and Defeat the U.S. Aggressors and All Their Running Dogs!" New China News Agency, May 20, 1970.
[62] Cf. R. Waring Herrick, "Soviet Charges of Sino-U.S. Collusion Appraised," Radio Liberty Dispatch, July 9, 1970.
[63] New China News Agency dispatch, January 2, 1970.
[64] Paul Wohl in Christian Science Monitor, January 7, 1970.
[65] Cf. John Hughes in Christian Science Monitor, January 7, 1970.
[66] See, e.g., Col. I. Makarov, "Militarist Hysteria in China," Red Star, March 31, 1970.
[67] Cf. S. Tikhvinsky, "Geopolitical Fortune Telling," Pravda, February 15, 1970; for commentary see Christian Duevel, "Tikhvinsky Denies Soviet Preemptive War Plans Against China," Radio Liberty Dispatch, February 23, 1970. Tikhvinsky is a member of the Soviet delegation to the Peking border talks.
[68] Cf. Bernard Gwertzman in New York Times, March 1, 1970.

and Pamir regions. There were even reports of an unpublicized agreement on a ceasefire and mutual troop withdrawal; [69] it appeared later, however, that these had been misleading. Reports also began to circulate that Moscow had decided to appoint V. I. Stepakov, who had just been relieved as head of the CPSU Central Committee's Propaganda and Agitation Department, as its ambassador to Peking,[70] and Moscow gave the impression that Peking had accepted him.[71] Ultimately, however, Stepakov's name was withdrawn, probably because Peking regarded him as discredited and without influence. (He was subsequently appointed ambassador to Yugoslavia.) Instead, it was the relatively important V. S. Tolstikov who arrived as Moscow's new ambassador to Peking on October 10.[72] By July it was known that Peking had appointed Deputy Foreign Minister Liu Hsin-ch'üan as its ambassador to the Soviet Union; he arrived in Moscow on November 23.[73] It also became known in July that Kuznetsov, who was evidently ill, would be replaced by Deputy Foreign Minister L. F. Ilyichev, who arrived in Peking in mid-August.[74]

In spite of the continuation of ideological and political polemics,[75] there were further signs in the late spring of 1970 of an improved climate of Sino-Soviet relations in general, mainly on account of the Cambodian crisis.[76] The main exception, apart from ideological questions, was the border talks themselves, which both Brezhnev [77] and Kosygin [78] pronounced more or less stalemated; at the same time they insisted that the Soviet Union would continue the talks, that it wanted

[69] Murrey Marder in *Washington Post,* April 16, 1970.

[70] Cf. r.r.g. (Richard Rockingham Gill), "The New Soviet Ambassador to Peking," Radio Free Europe Research Paper, April 2, 1970.

[71] Cf. Charlotte Saikowski in *Christian Science Monitor,* July 20, 1970.

[72] New China News Agency dispatch, October 10, 1970.

[73] New China News Agency dispatch, November 22, 1970.

[74] See note 70 and Bernard Gwertzman in *New York Times,* August 16, 1970.

[75] See, e.g., "Leninism or Social Imperialism?" *People's Daily, Red Flag,* and *Liberation Army Daily,* April 22, 1970; "Pseudorevolutionaries with the Mask Off," *Pravda,* May 18, 1970.

[76] Cf. Anthony Astrachan in *Washington Post,* May 10, 1970; Paul Wohl in *Christian Science Monitor,* May 22, 1970. Kosygin said in a press conference of May 4 that the Cambodian crisis made unity among "socialist" countries more imperative than ever (Anthony Astrachan in *Washington Post,* May 19, 1970).

[77] Speech in Alma Ata, August 28, 1970 (Radio Moscow, August 28, 1970).

[78] Speech of June 10, 1970 (cf. Bernard Gwertzman in *New York Times,* June 11, 1970); interview with editor Edatata Narayanan of the New Delhi *Patriot,* August 10, 1970.

an improvement of relations between the two states, and that it would not attack China; Brezhnev, the major figure in the Soviet leadership, was less positive in tone than was Kosygin. The powerful Soviet military buildup near the Chinese frontier, to a level of approximately thirty-five divisions, had been continuing while the talks were in progress.[79] The Chinese Army Day editorial displayed an exaggerated sensitivity to the buildup.[80] In reality, the tension along the border itself appears to have eased, in spite of the Soviet buildup.[81] As of the summer of 1970, the border talks appeared to be stalemated in a series of arguments over the historical basis of territorial claims on both sides.[82] Moscow announced a campaign to colonize a disputed island near Khabarovsk, at the confluence of the Amur and Ussuri rivers.[83] At the end of the year, the two sides disagreed flatly as to whether the annual round of border river navigation talks just concluded had produced agreement; Moscow asserted that it had,[84] Peking that it had not.[85]

At about the same time, Chou En-lai told the American journalist Edgar Snow that China still felt threatened by the Soviet Union, as well as by the United States and Japan. As for the situation along the Sino-Soviet border, he added, in Snow's words, that "In practice, it seems, the Russians have simply refused to agree to disengage in the disputed areas, where the two lines remain as intertwined as the prongs of two forks pushed together." [86]

It is evident that the Peking talks on the Sino-Soviet border question made little substantive progress during the first eighteen months. To any one with even a slight familiarity with the history of Soviet and Chinese Communist negotiating techniques, this should not be surprising. It appears that only a marked improvement in the basic political relationship between the two sides or a resumption of effective military threats and pressures by the Soviet Union has much chance of pro-

[79] William Beecher in *New York Times,* July 22, 1970.

[80] "Heighten Vigilance, Defend the Motherland," *People's Daily, Red Flag,* and *Liberation Army Daily,* August 1, 1970.

[81] See second source cited in note 39.

[82] Cf. r.r.g. (Richard Rockingham Gill), "History to the Aid of Soviet Borders," Radio Free Europe Research Paper, August 25, 1970.

[83] Henry S. Hayward in *Christian Science Monitor,* August 14, 1970.

[84] Henry S. Hayward in *Christian Science Monitor,* December 24, 1970.

[85] New China News Agency dispatch, December 23, 1970.

[86] Edgar Snow, "Talks with Chou En-lai: The Open Door," *The New Republic,* March 27, 1971, pp. 22-23.

ducing rapid progress toward a settlement. The outlook for these alternative developments is discussed in Chapter 4. It is clear that one of several powerful disincentives on the Soviet side to a resumption of threats and pressures, let alone an actual major military attack, is the realization that China has shown itself capable of fighting a "people's war" if compelled to do so.

# 3

# Peking's Political and Military Response to the Crisis

The Chinese side, like the Soviet side, of the Sino-Soviet border crisis interacted strongly with domestic politics. The present chapter examines this interaction.

It is important to realize that, although Maoist sources speak of "two lines" in the recent history of the Chinese Communist movement—those of Mao Tse-tung on the one hand and the allegedly "revisionist" Liu Shao-ch'i on the other—three major leadership groups have actually been involved. They have been led and best represented by Mao Tse-tung, Liu Shao-ch'i, and Chou En-lai and may be labeled respectively the Maoists, the party managers, and the administrators. The first group believes fervently in Mao's "mass line" of popular mobilization through slogans and ideological appeals, as well as in all other aspects of his "thought"; on occasion this group, which includes some members like Mao's wife Chiang Ching who are even more militant than the Chairman himself, has pushed the "mass line" to extremes, of which the most notable have been the Great Leap Forward and the Cultural Revolution. The second group has been basically opposed to extreme application of the "mass line" and has preferred a more Leninist system of party apparatus controls over the political system and the population. The third group, which includes some military elements, has usually been willing, for a variety of reasons, including a desire to reduce the inconvenient influence of the party apparatus, to support the first group when it has been involved in a dispute with the second but has tried to restrain the Maoists from indulging in the extreme aspects of their "line."

51

From a purely political standpoint, the Cultural Revolution represented a victory of the first and third groups over the second. The cooperation of the third group was essential to the Maoists during the Cultural Revolution and has remained essential ever since; but this cooperation has not prevented policy differences and debates between them.[1]

One of these differences related to the Red Guards, the chosen instrument of the Maoists for the prosecution of the Cultural Revolution; the administrators saw the Red Guards as threatening the country with chaos and probably argued that they should be brought under control. By late July 1968, the Red Guards had created such disorder that Mao himself felt reluctantly compelled to authorize the army—which had increasingly assumed the responsibility for local administration since early 1967—to begin the suppression of the Red Guards as an organized political force.[2] For all practical purposes this turn to the right meant the end of the Cultural Revolution.

## The Political Situation on the Eve of the Ussuri Clashes

At the Twelfth Plenary Session of the party Central Committee (October 13-31, 1968), Maoists and administrators debated inconclusively the proper political course for the future, while apparently agreeing to push ahead with the rebuilding of the party from the wreckage left by the Cultural Revolution and hold the Ninth Party Congress as soon as feasible.[3] The new draft of the party constitution adopted at the Twelfth Plenary Session extolled Mao and named Lin Piao as his successor, but failed to specify that the army should be under the control of the party.[4] The main interest of the third group was the restoration of domestic order and stability as soon as possible—which implied relatively forceful

---

[1] Cf. Philip L. Bridgham, "The Cultural Revolution and the New Political System in China," a paper presented at the annual meeting of the American Political Science Association, Los Angeles, September 1970.

[2] The theoretical rationale for this step was given in an important article by Yao Wen-yuan (a leading member of the Maoist group), "The Working Class Must Exercise Leadership in Everything," *Red Flag*, no. 2 (August 1968). See Richard Baum, "China: the Year of the Mangoes," *Asian Survey*, vol. ix, no. 1 (January 1969), pp. 1-17; John Gittings, "Revolutionary See-saw," *Far Eastern Economic Review*, October 3, 1968, pp. 14-17.

[3] Cf. John Gittings, "Peking Walls Have Ears Too," *Far Eastern Economic Review*, January 30, 1969, pp. 175-176.

[4] The text of the draft constitution was published in *New York Times*, January 8, 1969.

methods; Premier Chou En-lai appears to have regarded the Soviet threat as an urgent argument for domestic stabilization.[5]

In the post-Cultural Revolution period, which for practical purposes began after the Twelfth Plenary Session, the politically surviving Maoists—although not so much Mao himself—tried to carry on much as before; ascendancy in policymaking, however, tended to pass to an emerging coalition of non-Maoists of which the administrators and many of the military leaders were the core, and which may be labeled the moderates.

Drastic policies were enforced in the last few months of 1968 and the first few months of 1969, mainly in the interest of stability; these comprised a massive transfer of 20-30 million people (including many former Red Guards) from the cities to the countryside to ease the pressures on the urban sector,[6] the reimposition of pre-Cultural Revolution controls on the peasantry,[7] substantial troop transfers to mitigate tensions between soldiers and populace that had arisen during the Cultural Revolution,[8] and tighter restrictions on periodicals and news available to foreigners.[9]

This heavyhanded domestic policy aroused intense opposition from Maoists both at the center and in the provinces.[10] Even Chou En-lai may have believed that military influence on domestic politics had become excessive.[11] The Maoists received powerful support when Mao

---

[5] Chou En-lai's National Day speech (New China News Agency dispatch, September 30, 1968) dwelt at some length on the threat and the need for war preparedness, in an essentially military vein rather than in one of exploiting the threat for purposes of domestic political mobilization. Lin Piao, who made the other major speech (New China News Agency dispatch, October 1, 1968) on that occasion, referred only very briefly to the threat and to the need for war preparedness.

[6] Tillman Durdin in *New York Times,* December 1, 1968; Stanley Karnow in *Washington Post,* February 21, 1969.

[7] Tillman Durdin in *New York Times,* December 15, 1968.

[8] Tillman Durdin in *The Times* (London), February 5, 1969.

[9] Tillman Durdin in *New York Times,* November 14, 1968. For a summary of the moderates' program see Stanley Karnow in *Washington Post,* January 9, 1969.

[10] Cf. Joseph C. Kun, "The Cultural Revolution: Trends and Prospects," Radio Free Europe Research Paper, January 9, 1969; Joseph C. Kun, "New Instances of Maoist 'Revolutionary Romanticism,' " Radio Free Europe Research Paper, February 10, 1969.

[11] The New Year's Day editorial ("Place Mao Tse-tung's Thought in Command of Everything," *People's Daily, Red Flag,* and *Liberation Army Daily,* January 1, 1969) placed much less stress on the role of the army than had the corresponding editorial of the year before.

himself returned to active public life in January 1969. The military rally held by Mao on January 25 (Chapter 2) signaled an intensified effort by the Maoists to affect the course of policy. Publicity was promptly given to the previously more or less dormant, but once powerful, Military Affairs Commission of the party Central Committee—of which Lin Piao serves as the active chairman—presumably to help promote Maoist influence on the army.[12] Economic policy, of special importance to Chou En-lai, was set on the basis of a compromise—labeled with the familiar expression "walking on two legs"—between the Maoist stress on local initiative inspired by Mao's "thought" and Chou's preference for more orthodox approaches.[13]

One of the results of this new, more Maoist, political atmosphere was the cancellation on February 19, 1969 of the invitation to the United States (Chapter 2) to resume the Warsaw talks. Another was a series of editorials attacking Soviet policy, including Soviet domestic policy.[14] Given this political atmosphere and the approach of the Ninth Party Congress, as well as developments on the Soviet side of the border, it is entirely possible that Maoist elements in the army organized the first Ussuri clash as a means of proclaiming the validity of the Maoist dual (anti-American and anti-Soviet) strategy, including "people's war," and in the hope of promoting favorable political changes in other countries, including the Soviet Union itself. The Soviet writer Konstantin Simonov may have been correct when he later attributed personal responsibility for the first Ussuri clash to Lin Piao.[15]

### The Policy Debate Following the Clashes

While Chou En-lai handled the diplomatic aftermath of the clash, the propaganda exploitation, which included demonstrations against the Soviet embassy in the Cultural Revolution manner, was wholly Maoist. It gave no indication that special measures of war preparedness were needed, presumably on the theory that such measures might strengthen the army's domestic political influence; in any case a Soviet attack could

---

[12] Cf. *People's Daily,* January 25, 1969.

[13] Cf. "Grasp Revolution, Promote Production and Win New Victories on the Industrial Front," *People's Daily,* February 21, 1969.

[14] See, e.g., "Soviet Revisionist Renegade Clique Finds Going Tougher and Tougher," New China News Agency, January 31, 1969.

[15] Konstantin Simonov, "Thinking Out Loud," *Pravda,* May 3, 1969.

be beaten through the Maoist strategy of "people's war." [16] The crisis began to be exploited as a means of promoting Maoist domestic policies.[17] Anti-Soviet propaganda of the Maoist variety continued after the second Ussuri clash, although it was somewhat less strident.[18]

The unusual length of the Ninth Party Congress (April 1-24) indicates that it was marked by considerable debate. There can be little doubt that domestic issues and policy toward the Soviet Union were among the main questions debated.[19] Lin Piao's political report, the major document presented to the congress, was delivered on April 1 [20] but not adopted until April 14, when it was announced that "The delegates have made many good proposals for additions and revisions of the report." [21] The published version [22] represented something of a compromise between the Maoist and moderate viewpoints; for the important question of war preparedness, for example, the published report gave both the Maoist, political rationale (for domestic mobilization) and the moderate, military rationale (for defense). On the whole, however, the outcome of the congress, as specifically represented in the composition of the new Central Committee, was an improvement in the relative political position of the moderates (including their powerful military component),[23] even though the final version of the new party constitution,[24] unlike the draft, stated that the army was to be subject to the leadership of the party. Since that time the political fortunes of the military members of the Central Committee, considered as a group, have prospered considerably better than those of the civilians, especially the Maoist civilians.[25]

---

[16] Cf. "Down with the New Tsars!" *People's Daily* and *Liberation Army Daily*, March 4, 1969; also other documents collected in "Sino-Soviet Border Clashes," *Current Background* (American Consulate General, Hong Kong), no. 876 (April 11, 1969).

[17] "On Summing Up Experience," *Red Flag*, nos. 3 and 4 (March 1969); text released by New China News Agency on March 14, 1969.

[18] See, e.g., "Revisionist New Tsars in Moscow are Chief Anti-Soviet Criminals," *People's Daily*, March 25, 1969.

[19] Cf. Peter Grose in *New York Times*, April 5, 1969.

[20] New China News Agency dispatch, April 1, 1969.

[21] New China News Agency dispatch, April 14, 1969.

[22] Text released by New China News Agency, April 27, 1969.

[23] Charles Mohr in *New York Times*, April 26, 1969.

[24] Text released by New China News Agency, April 28, 1969.

[25] Cf. "The Party Central Committee Today," *China News Analysis* (Hong Kong), no. 832 (February 19, 1971).

During the succeeding months the Chinese press was filled with a wave of articles, mostly by obscure Maoists, denouncing many aspects of Soviet domestic and foreign policy, including its handling of the border dispute and its alleged "collusion" with the United States to "encircle" China.[26] It was reasonably clear that both the Maoists and the moderates were trying to use the tension with the Soviet Union as a rationale for their own preferred domestic policies. The essence of the Maoist line in this context was that "unity with the masses" and other manifestations of Maoist behavior by the army were the best defense against possible aggression by the Soviet Union (or allegedly by the United States); an example is a passage from a major editorial of June 8: [27]

> . . . we should abide by Chairman Mao's teaching: 'We will not attack unless we are attacked; if we are attacked, we will certainly counterattack,' and seriously deal with the plots of aggression of U.S. imperialism, Soviet revisionism and all reaction, and make preparations against their launching a big war and against their launching a conventional war and against their launching a large-scale nuclear war. The great unity of the whole party, the whole army and the people of the whole country on the basis of Mao Tsetung thought is a sure guarantee that we will fulfill our fighting tasks and defeat our common enemies.

The major pronouncements on Army Day (August 1) revealed two of the major differences between the Maoists and the moderates. These were the insistence by the Maoists that the army must conduct itself in accordance with Maoist principles, rather than stressing order and stability for their own sakes as the moderates would prefer, when dealing with the populace, and that such behavior would be the best means of preparing the country to fight a "people's war" if necessary; and the more provocative attitude and language of the Maoists where the Soviet Union was concerned. The major editorial on this occasion [28] asserted that the army's "ties with the masses" and its "consciousness of

---

26 "Hold Aloft the Banner of Unity of the Party's Ninth Congress and Win Still Greater Victories," *People's Daily, Red Flag,* and *Liberation Army Daily,* June 8, 1969. The formula "Mao Tse-tung thought" has been standard in the New China News Agency's English language transmissions since the Ninth Party Congress.

27 A sample is included in " 'Soviet Revisionist Social-Imperialism' and 'US-Soviet Collaboration,' " *Current Background,* no. 883 (June 26, 1969).

28 "The People's Army is Invincible," *People's Daily, Red Flag,* and *Liberation Army Daily,* August 1, 1969.

class struggle, were "the best way of building the army and of getting prepared against war," and it referred repeatedly to "Soviet revisionist social-imperialism." Chief of Staff Huang Yung-sheng's speech,[29] on the other hand, referred to war preparedness in almost purely military terms and refrained from prefixing "social-imperialism" and "revisionism" with the word Soviet.

Meanwhile, it was clear that the legacy of the Cultural Revolution, including struggles between Maoists and moderates (notably military personnel), was causing serious disorder in many of the provinces— a particularly disturbing phenomenon to the central leadership on account of the Soviet threat. The situation was especially serious in the border provinces; and a Central Committee directive of August 28 to the Revolutionary Committees and military authorities of these provinces stressed the urgency of war preparedness and the restoration of order, although in Maoist language.[30]

The Kosygin visit of September 11, 1969, which the extreme Maoists probably opposed, and the proposals he brought from Russia presented the divided Chinese leadership with a major policy problem. The militant and extremely anti-Soviet tone of the National Day slogans, which were published on September 16,[31] provides probably the best clue to the early progress of the debate and suggests strongly that the Maoists were objecting to the idea of yielding to "social-imperialism" to the extent of holding the talks the Soviet Union was demanding. The National Day (October 1) speeches of Lin Piao [32] and Chou En-lai,[33] however, were by Chinese standards relatively nonprovocative in their references to the Soviet Union. The National Day editorial [34] was somewhat more militant in its comments on the Soviet Union than were Lin and Chou's speeches, but it did not go so far as to tell the army that the best means of defending the country was to maintain "close ties with the masses." The press release [35] on a military rally held on October 14 and attended by the top leadership used only the

---

29 Text released by New China News Agency, August 1, 1969.

30 Cf. Stanley Karnow in *Washington Post,* August 29, 1969.

31 Text released by New China News Agency, September 16, 1969.

32 Text released by New China News Agency, October 1, 1969.

33 Text released by New China News Agency, September 30, 1969.

34 "Fight for the Further Consolidation of the Dictatorship of the Proletariat," *People's Daily, Red Flag,* and *Liberation Army Daily,* October 1, 1969.

35 New China News Agency dispatch, October 14, 1969.

relatively inoffensive term "modern revisionism," rather than "social imperialism."

There was probably a minority of extreme Maoists, however, including Chiang Ching, who regarded the decision to go to the conference table as a form of appeasement likely to lower the fighting morale of the "revolutionary people" of China and the world and who favored instead a policy of militant confrontation. The five-month period following the Chou-Kosygin talks saw a wave of productions of and commentaries on "revolutionary" plays, operas, and films glorifying defiance of the enemy (whoever he might be) and "people's war." Probably the most publicized was the opera *Taking the Bandits' Stronghold,* which had originally been "revised" by Chiang Ching, and which was presented beginning in October 1969 in another "revised" version, again apparently under her auspices.[36] Some of the commentaries went so far as explicitly to advocate resistance in the event of attack by "imperialism" or "social-imperialism." [37] The implied attitude toward the Soviet Union and the Peking talks was strongly hostile. It was clear, however, that the decision to hold the talks was not to be reversed by these means. At the end of November Chou En-lai made a speech in which he hardly alluded to the Soviet Union or to the SALT talks, which had just begun, and not at all to the Peking talks; he concentrated instead on attacking the "intensified military collusion" between the United States and Japan allegedly represented by the Nixon-Sato talks.[38] It is possible that Chou felt a sense of relief at being able credibly to hold up these two targets, which all sections of the Chinese leadership could agree on denouncing, instead of the Soviet Union.

### The War Preparedness Campaign [39]

The war preparedness campaign began in the autumn of 1969. It was a complex affair related not only to the Soviet threat but to other aspects of Chinese foreign policy and—perhaps still more important—

---

[36] Text in *Red Flag,* no. 11 (October 29, 1969) (see *Survey of China Mainland Magazines* [American Consulate General, Hong Kong], no. 668 [December 1, 1969]). Some commentaries on this work are collected in *Current Background,* no. 898 (December 22, 1969).

[37] See, e.g., Hung Ch'eng (pseud.), "Let's See Who in the World Can Match Us," *People's Daily,* October 16, 1969.

[38] New China News Agency dispatch, November 29, 1969.

[39] This section draws heavily on Lü Yung-shu, "Preparations for War in Mainland China," a paper presented at the First Sino-American Conference on Mainland China, Taipei, Taiwan, December 1970.

58

to domestic policy. The approach to analyzing the campaign adopted here is to describe briefly the major categories of measures connected with it, to construct a rationale for the campaign as a whole, and to consider its outcome.

Beginning in the summer of 1969, a northward movement of Chinese troops, of substantial size, was effected. It included four divisions moved near the Manchurian frontier and six divisions moved into Inner Mongolia.[40] The greater part of Inner Mongolia was divided for military purposes among the adjacent Mukden, Peking, and Lanchow Military Regions, probably to facilitate defense in depth by locating the command and control centers farther to the rear.[41] An elaborate program of defensive military construction was undertaken in the border regions;[42] and the intake of conscripts into the armed forces was substantially increased.[43] Extensive civil defense measures (digging of air raid shelters, partial evacuation of cities) was initiated in many parts of China, including areas as remote from the Soviet frontier as Kwangtung.[44] An expansion and upgrading (of equipment, training, and so on) of the militia was begun under the army's auspices. An obvious effort was made to regain the momentum for the military modernization program that had been largely lost during the Cultural Revolution, without being overly provocative toward the Soviet Union; some Indian reports alleged the dispersal of certain defense industries and even, rather implausibly, the transfer of some nuclear installations from Sinkiang to Tibet.[45] Much emphasis was placed on the danger of war as a rationale for economic, and especially industrial, decentralization.[46] Grain stockpiling was emphasized [47] under the slogan, "Be prepared against war, be prepared against natural disasters, and do everything for

---

[40] *Ibid.,* p. 5.
[41] Tillman Durdin in *New York Times,* June 21, 1970; Paul Hyer, "The China-Mongol Frontier: The Cultural Revolution and After," a paper presented at the First Sino-American Conference on Mainland China, Taipei, Taiwan, December 1970.
[42] Lü, *op. cit.,* pp. 6-7.
[43] *Ibid.,* p. 12.
[44] Tillman Durdin in *New York Times,* November 21, 1969; Lü, *op. cit.,* p. 17.
[45] Ernest Weatherall in *Christian Science Monitor,* March 13, 1970. The army apparently did not take part in gathering the 1969 harvest (John Hughes in *Christian Science Monitor,* December 4, 1969).
[46] See, e.g., "The Road to China's Socialist Industrialization," *Red Flag,* no. 10 (September 30, 1969); Stanley Karnow in *Washington Post,* October 15, 1969.
[47] Cf. New China News Agency dispatch, July 13, 1969; Lü, *op. cit.,* p. 22.

the people." To some extent, stockpiling of strategic raw materials, such as steel and rubber, was initiated at about the time of the semi-annual Canton international trade fair of October 1969. Great emphasis was placed on increasing industrial production.[48]

It is evident that, although the war preparedness campaign was conducted with special energy in the regions bordering the Soviet Union and to a considerable extent was actually evoked by the Soviet threat, it was a nationwide effort with a broader rationale. The year 1969 was a period not only of the maximum Soviet threat to date but of serious post-Cultural Revolution disorder, notably between the military and Maoist elements in the provinces, and of natural disasters. A conjunction of domestic and external difficulties perceived by the leadership as a threat was exaggerated for popular consumption through propaganda and used to promote domestic and external measures regarded as desirable. Maoist and non-Maoist elements of the central and provincial elites evidently regarded the situation differently and engaged in a competitive effort to turn the war preparedness campaign to partisan advantage.

A reasonable reconstruction of the Maoist effort might begin with the Maoists' psychological and ideological need to compensate themselves somehow for the holding of the Peking talks with the detested Soviet "revisionists" and for the partial deescalation of the cult of Mao Tse-tung beginning in July 1969; [49] for this purpose the war preparedness campaign offered a useful distraction and outlet. The Maoists were also eager to prepare for a genuine "people's war" in the event of invasion by the Soviet Union or the United States or India, or some combination of these, or, better still, to deter an invasion by demonstrating that China was no Czechoslovakia. The Soviet Union, the United States, and India represented, of course, the threefold demonology of "imperialism, modern revisionism, and reaction," which had figured regularly in Maoist pronouncements since the critical Tenth Plenary Session of the Eighth Central Committee in September 1962.[50] To some Maoists the war preparedness campaign may have appeared

---

[48] Lü, *op. cit.*, pp. 22-23.

[49] There is reason to believe that Mao himself had grown weary of the lengths to which the cult of his "thought" had been pushed during the Cultural Revolution (cf. Edgar Snow, "A Conversation with Mao Tse-tung," *Life*, April 30, 1970, pp. 46-47).

[50] See text of communique of Tenth Plenary Session released by New China News Agency, September 28, 1962.

as a possible method of stimulating, by example and without maintaining a dangerous posture of direct confrontation, the emergence elsewhere of "people's wars" against China's adversaries; in 1958, similarly, the unsuccessful strategy of direct confrontation with "imperialism" in the Taiwan Strait had given way to indirect encouragement of anti-"imperialist" struggles by the "revolutionary people of the world" against the American "paper tiger." [51] At home, the Maoists probably hoped that the war preparedness campaign would enhance the political influence of Lin Piao and the political apparatus of the armed forces as a counterweight to the predominantly non-Maoist provincial military leaderships; [52] the campaign would also help to break up the "independent kingdoms" of some of the provincial military leaders by transferring certain of their units to other parts of the country. In Kwangtung war preparations were intense, and this may have reflected a Maoist desire to weaken the "independent kingdom" of the moderate Huang Yung-sheng, who had commanded the Canton Military Region before becoming chief of staff in 1968. It is clear that the Maoists, and Mao himself, also intended to use the war preparedness campaign, which emphasized local initiative, to enhance their favorite principle of economic decentralization and local self-reliance in nearly everything.[53]

On the non-Maoist side, there was also of course a determination to prepare against a possible Soviet attack; less concern was probably felt for the United States and India, both of which were being por-

---

[51] Cf. "Comrade Mao Tse-tung on 'Imperialism and All Reactionaries Are Paper Tigers,' " *People's Daily,* October 27, 1958.

[52] The appointment of Li Te-sheng, Chairman of the Anhui Revolutionary Committee and an Alternate Politburo member, as Director of the General Political Department of the People's Liberation Army General Staff was revealed by the New China News Agency on September 2, 1970; Chiang Ching's influence has been strong in Anhui since the Cultural Revolution (Colina MacDougall, "A National People's Congress?" *Far Eastern Economic Review,* July 23, 1970, p. 22). On the growth of the Lin Piao cult see Norman Webster in *New York Times,* November 1, 1970.

[53] Cf. Mao's remark to the First Plenary Session of the Ninth Central Committee [April 28, 1969] ("Mao Tse-tung's Speech to the First Plenary Session of the CCP Ninth Central Committee," *Issues and Studies* [Taipei], vol. vi, no. 2 [November 1969], p. 92):

Next, I would like to talk about preparation for war. Don't ask the central authorities to distribute materials for manufacturing hand grenades. Most provinces can manufacture hand grenades and light weaponry on their own. This is material preparation. Mainly, we should have spiritual preparation and readiness to fight. When we are attacked we should retaliate. Experience has proven that we can deal with tanks and armoured vehicles.

trayed as active threats in Maoist propaganda. It seemed that the campaign could be conducted less provocatively at this time than before, since the Peking talks had begun; and yet, somewhat paradoxically, the preparations appeared necessary in part because the talks were not going well. The campaign probably appealed to the non-Maoists as a useful vehicle for promoting military modernization at a somewhat faster rate than had been possible during the confusion of the Cultural Revolution. It could also be used to counter both the Maoist tendency to charge that the Peking talks were a form of appeasement and even betrayal, and any possible Maoist demand for the dangerous step of repudiating the alliance with the Soviet Union, as Albania had done in September 1969. Most important of all, the non-Maoists wanted to enhance and institutionalize their already predominant influence at the provincial level, to increase their ability to control the process of rebuilding the provincial party apparatuses, and to enlarge their representation in the governmental bureaucracy, which was also in process of reconstruction.

As between the two sides, the non-Maoists gained the greater advantage from the war preparedness campaign. The Peking talks were not disrupted by the campaign, and the moderates gained increased influence at the provincial level and in the reemerging governmental bureaucracy.[54] Maoist influence remained strong, however, in some areas such as Shanghai, as well as at the center, where it benefited from the prestige of Mao himself and certain of his supporters, including Chiang Ching.[55]

As though by tacit agreement between the two sides, the war preparedness campaign was re-intensified in the summer and autumn of 1970, with greater relative emphasis on the alleged threat of attack by the United States and Japan. The Soviet Union was not ignored in this connection, but there was a noticeable tendency to stress it less than before and to use the term "social-imperialism" without the provocative prefix "Soviet." At the Second Plenary Session of the Ninth Central Committee (August 23-September 6, 1970), the Military Affairs Commission, whose active chairman is Lin Piao, presented an unpublished report on the war preparedness campaign.[56] In the latter months of

[54] Cf. Tillman Durdin in *New York Times*, September 29, 1970; j.c.k. (Joseph C. Kun), "Leadership Trends in Peking and the Provinces," Radio Free Europe Research Paper, June 2, 1970.
[55] Cf. MacDougall, *loc. cit.*, p. 22.
[56] Text of communique released by New China News Agency, September 9, 1970.

1970 the Maoist element of the central leadership was weakened by the disappearance and possible purging of the radical ideologue Ch'en Po-ta, a member of the Politburo Standing Committee. As suggested by the fact that his last public appearance was on Army Day (August 1), he probably fell victim to the army's disfavor.[57] The probability that by that time the war preparedness campaign had acquired a stronger domestic, as opposed to external, motivation than ever is indicated by the fact that it tended to taper off toward the end of the year,[58] as provincial Party Committees, under predominantly military control like the Revolutionary Committees, began to be formed.[59] The war scare and the war preparedness campaign, in short, seem to have fallen off not only in proportion as the threat from the Soviet Union has declined, but as the domestic political situation has tended to stabilize in favor of the non-Maoist, and especially the military, element of the leadership.

[57] Cf. j.c.k. (Joseph C. Kun), "Leadership Lineup Reveals Possible New Policies," Radio Free Europe Research Paper, October 1, 1970.

[58] The New Year's Day editorial ("Advance Victoriously Along Chairman Mao's Revolutionary Line," People's Daily, Red Flag, and Liberation Army Daily, January 1, 1971), Maoist as always, stressed alleged revolutionary trends in the world at large and said very little about any direct threat to China and the war preparedness campaign.

[59] Cf. j.c.k. (Joseph C. Kun), "Party Consolidation Leads to Emergence of New Strong Men," Radio Free Europe Research Paper, January 12, 1971; j.c.k., "Party 'Reconstruction' in Full Swing," Radio Free Europe Research Paper, February 2, 1971; Lee Lescaze in Washington Post, February 20, 1971.

# 4

# Current Problems and the Future of Sino-Soviet Relations

It is clear that during 1970 the chances of war between China and the Soviet Union diminished, although not necessarily to zero, but that Sino-Soviet relations continued to be chilly in the state field and hostile in the party field. This chapter explores the major current issues that appear to account for this coolness, as a preliminary to a consideration of the outlook for Sino-Soviet relations.

## Bilateral State Relations

After receiving a Soviet ambassador (V. S. Tolstikov), and shortly before sending an ambassador of its own (Liu Hsin-ch'üan) to Moscow, Peking used the occasion of the October Revolution anniversary in 1970 to send an unusually conciliatory message to Moscow. For the first time in a major Chinese document, it is explicitly stated, as Soviet sources had already done several times, that "differences of principle" (i.e., ideological and major political issues) should not be allowed to impede the development of "normal state relations"; these relations, Peking as usual interpreted as being conducted on the basis of the Five Principles of Peaceful Coexistence.[1] It is possible that the sending of this message was facilitated by the previous disappearance of the Maoist Ch'en Po-ta from public view and his possible dropping from the Politburo Standing Committee.[2] It may also be significant that another reputedly doctrinaire member of the Standing Committee, K'ang Sheng, who had been concerned with Peking's relations with foreign Communist parties and might

---

[1] Text released by New China News Agency, November 6, 1970.

[2] Cf. j.c.k. (Joseph C. Kun), "Chinese Overture to the Soviet Union," Radio Free Europe Research Paper, November 9, 1970.

have been expected to oppose the sending of such a message, also disappeared from public view for six months after attending a reception for President Yahya Khan of Pakistan on November 13, 1970. Except for one deletion (a reference to Stalin) the Chinese message was published in the Soviet press; otherwise, the Soviet treatment of Sino-Soviet relations on the 1970 October Revolution anniversary consisted mainly of a statement by M. A. Suslov of the CPSU secretariat, the major speaker, to the effect that despite ideological differences and the slow progress of the Peking talks, Moscow was doing its best to normalize its relations with Peking in the state sphere. Suslov detracted somewhat from the impression created by these remarks, however, by saying that the Soviet armed forces would be equipped with the "most modern weapons" in order to enable them to strike a "shattering blow at anyone who sought to encroach on the holy borders of the fatherland." [3]

The annual Sino-Soviet talks on border river navigation seem to have been especially difficult in 1970, probably as a reflection of the slow progress of the border talks in Peking. The former began in July,[4] but it was not until December 20 that the Soviet side announced their successful completion.[5] Peking promptly denied that any agreement had been reached, except for one to meet again in 1971.[6]

A Sino-Soviet trade agreement was signed on November 23, 1970, thereby perhaps halting a decline of several years' duration that had reduced China to the rank of the Soviet Union's least important trading partner among the Communist countries.[7] Although no details were published, there were indications that a substantial expansion in trade was planned for 1971,[8] and that some elements of the Chinese military, possibly to the displeasure of certain of their civilian colleagues, might be interested in obtaining spare parts for military equipment, particularly jet fighters that had been acquired from the Soviet Union in earlier years.[9]

---

[3] Anthony Astrachan in *Washington Post,* November 7, 1970; Paul Wohl in *Christian Science Monitor,* November 19, 1970.

[4] Tass dispatch, July 10, 1970.

[5] Henry S. Hayward in *Christian Science Monitor,* December 24, 1970.

[6] New China News Agency dispatch, December 23, 1970.

[7] j.c.k. (Joseph C. Kun), "Steps Toward Normalization of Trade Relations," Radio Free Europe Research Paper, March 3, 1971.

[8] Bernard Gwertzman in *New York Times,* March 24, 1971.

[9] Cf. *Christian Science Monitor,* October 22, 1970; j.c.k. (Joseph C. Kun), "Reemergence of the 'Bourgeois Military Line?'" Radio Free Europe Research Paper, January 19, 1971.

If an examination of the major bilateral issues indicates a moderately favorable prospect for an improvement of Sino-Soviet relations in the state field, the prospect becomes less favorable when issues involving third countries are taken into account.

## Third Country Issues

There are three main third countries or areas where Chinese and Soviet national interests tend to conflict. These are the United States, Asia, and Eastern Europe. Since the relationship of the United States to the Sino-Soviet dispute is discussed in Chapter 5, it will be omitted here.

Peking is highly suspicious and resentful of growing Soviet activity in Asia and is far from mollified by Soviet assurances that Moscow would welcome China into its proposed "Asian security system." [10] On the whole, however, the Soviet Union probably has even greater reason to be concerned over China's activities in Asia: Since the beginning of its normalization campaign, Peking has been highly effective in enhancing its ties with and standing in Asia, in ways some of which clearly have anti-Soviet overtones.[11]

Since 1969, Peking has increased its political support for and its economic and military aid to North Vietnam, partly as a means of countering Soviet influence, which has been an object of its jealousy for many years. The latest manifestation of this policy was Chou En-lai's trip to Hanoi (March 5-8, 1971) at the time of the crisis created by the American-supported South Vietnamese invasion of southern Laos.[12] Although the Laotian situation was the ostensible reason for the visit, another probable purpose was to dissuade Hanoi from sending a delegation to the Soviet Twenty-fourth Party Congress. If so, the visit was a failure in this respect, since Hanoi sent a delegation.[13] Another purpose may have been to indicate to Hanoi that Peking was not to be deterred by developments in Indochina from improving its relationships with the American "people" if not with the United States government.

---

[10] Cf. r.r.g. (Richard Rockingham Gill), "China Offered a Place in Brezhnev's Asian Security System," Radio Free Europe Research Paper, September 24, 1970.

[11] See the excellent summary by Tillman Durdin in New York Times, May 11, 1970.

[12] Cf. joint communique (text released by New China News Agency, March 10, 1971).

[13] Cf. j.c.k. (Joseph C. Kun), "Continued Tightrope Walking in Hanoi," Radio Free Europe Research Paper, March 26, 1971.

Peking has similarly wooed North Korea, also with a partly anti-Soviet purpose. For example, in early March 1970 Pyongyang withdrew from a project of oceanographic cooperation with the Soviet Union because Moscow wanted to include Japanese scientists in the project; this action opened the way to the sending of a Chinese ambassador to Pyongyang and to a visit by Chou En-lai early in April. Late in June Peking capitalized on the twentieth anniversaries of the outbreak of the Korean War (June 25) and the beginning of the American "occupation" of Taiwan (June 27) by sending to Pyongyang a high level delegation under Chief of Staff Huang Yung-sheng.[14] It was apparently at this time that Peking privately agreed to drop a small territorial claim against North Korea that it had been maintaining for some years.[15] It also increased its economic and technical aid to North Korea following an agreement signed in October 1970.[16] North Korea, however, like North Vietnam, stood in too great a need of Soviet aid and support, as a counterweight both to the United States (and perhaps Japan) and to China, to follow Peking too far in denouncing the Soviet Union or otherwise jeopardizing its ties with Moscow. Again, like North Vietnam, it sent a high ranking delegation to the Soviet Twenty-fourth Congress, as both had to the Twenty-third (March 1966).

Both China and the Soviet Union have serious disputes with Japan and feel some nervousness over the possibility of Japanese rearmament in the context of potential American disengagement from Asia. For obvious geographic reasons, Peking has a more serious problem in this respect than does Moscow. For geographic, cultural, and historical reasons, on the other hand, Peking is better able than is Moscow to influence public opinion in Japan and indirectly its official policy. Trade, or the lure of trade, is one of China's main instruments in dealing with Japan. There is reason to believe that Moscow is somewhat concerned over the growth of Sino-Japanese trade and its possible tendency to reduce the Soviet Union's capacity for exerting political influence over Japan and economic influence over China.[17]

---

[14] Harold C. Hinton, *Communist China and the Problem of Korean Unification,* a paper presented at the International Conference on the Problems of Korean Unification, Seoul, Korea, August 1970; j.c.k. (Joseph C. Kun), "Cementing North Korean-Chinese Ties," Radio Free Europe Research Paper, April 9, 1970.

[15] *New York Times,* November 23, 1970.

[16] New China News Agency dispatch, October 17, 1970.

[17] Cf. "USSR Becoming Nervous About Japan-China Memorandum Trade Agreement, on Grounds of 'Support of China,'" *Mainichi* (Tokyo), April 20, 1970.

A probable recent example of the tendency for Peking's stand on Asian questions to differentiate itself as sharply as possible from Moscow's is provided by their contrasting reactions to the fighting in East Pakistan. Although Peking has a major political stake in good relations with Pakistan and is involved in a substantial program of economic and military aid to its government, it made rather ambiguous pronouncements for several days after the outbreak of the fighting in East Pakistan in March 1971 between elements of the local population and troops from West Pakistan.[18] Probably the Maoist principle of support for "revolutionary people" against oppressive governments was creating some sympathy for the cause of Bangla Desh (East Pakistan) in Peking. On the other hand, the possibility of a real "people's war" emerging in East Pakistan, and of Peking's being able to support it effectively if it did emerge, must have appeared slight, since the necessary conditions for one were not then present, and Peking probably also retained a painful memory of the fact that it had sided with Biafra to no avail. The final catalyst for Peking's ultimate decision may well have been not only Chinese suspicions of Indian intervention in East Pakistan but Soviet President Podgorny's appeal to President Yahya Khan to moderate the repression in East Pakistan. In any case, on April 11 Peking issued a statement supporting the Yahya government of East Pakistan and denouncing alleged American, Soviet, and Indian interference in its affairs.[19]

On the other hand, Soviet resentment of Chinese activity in Eastern Europe, especially in Albania, dates back about a decade. Peking regards Soviet efforts to dominate Eastern Europe not only as wrong in themselves but as dangerous precedents for the Sino-Soviet relationship. This attitude has been especially evident since Russia's invasion of Czechoslovakia. And Peking's apprehensions have been strengthened by Moscow's insistence, when renegotiating its bilateral treaties with its Warsaw Pact allies, on making the treaties applicable against "any state or group of states," instead of merely against a European enemy (presumably West Germany, with or without American support).[20] Peking is probably afraid, not so much that East European forces might actually fight against it in the event of a Sino-Soviet war, but that the revised treaties

---

[18] Cf. Lee Lescaze in *Washington Post,* April 11, 1971.

[19] Commentator, "What Are the Indian Expansionists Trying to Do?" *People's Daily,* April 11, 1971.

[20] Cf. R. Waring Herrick, "Brezhnev Builds a Bilateral Treaty Bulwark Against China," *Radio Liberty Dispatch,* May 20, 1970.

might facilitate Moscow's tendency to use the alleged Chinese menace in efforts to maintain Soviet influence in Eastern Europe, in proportion as fear of the West German menace gradually subsides, with Soviet charges of Sino-West German collusion serving as a kind of bridge between the two successive menaces.[21]

China is not the only objector to any such effort; Romania is another. The revised Soviet-Romanian treaty, signed on July 7, 1970, included the formula "any state or group of states" (Article 8), but Romania clearly refused to regard the treaty as being aimed at China.[22] The date of the treaty itself, which was the anniversary of the beginning of the Japanese invasion of China in 1937, may have been intended to remind Peking that under the Sino-Soviet alliance of 1950 Moscow was its protector against Japan. In any case, Moscow in a broadcast to the Chinese armed forces took pains to stress the positive aspects of the treaty and even seemed to imply that it might serve as a model for a reconstructed Sino-Soviet relationship.[23] During a visit to China a few weeks after the signing of the treaty, Romanian Defense Minister Ion Ionita seemingly stated what Bucharest considered to be the limits of its military obligations to the Soviet Union when he asserted that "In case *imperialism* launches aggression *in Europe,* socialist Romania will fulfill its duties as a Warsaw Treaty state." [24] In view of Romania's consistent refusal to be manipulated by Moscow for anti-Chinese purposes, it is not surprising that Peking agreed in March 1971 to begin a substantial program of industrial aid to Romania.[25]

Further causes of alarm occurred on August 12, 1970, when the Soviet-West German treaty was signed. This might be interpreted as an effort by Moscow to tidy up its western flank so that it could be free to renew military confrontation with China. A more realistic interpretation, and the one that evidently prevailed in Peking, was that whatever the main Soviet purpose in signing the treaty might have been, the result might be increased Soviet political exploitation of the China issue to

---

[21] On the latter point see R. Waring Herrick, "Soviet Charges of Sino-U.S. Collusion Appraised," *Radio Liberty Dispatch,* July 9, 1970.

[22] Cf. R. Waring Herrick, "Soviet and Rumanian Interpretations of Renewed Treaty Diverge on Key Issues," *Radio Liberty Dispatch,* August 13, 1970.

[23] Radio Moscow broadcast, July 9, 1970.

[24] New China News Agency dispatch, July 30, 1970. Emphasis added.

[25] j.c.k. (Joseph C. Kun), "Chinese to Build Complete Plants in Rumania," Radio Free Europe Research Paper, March 23, 1971.

compensate for the declining value of the German issue, and that Moscow had rendered itself vulnerable to propaganda attack. As it turned out, the opposite was the case if anything; the reception of the treaty in Eastern Europe was generally favorable, except in Albania, which explicitly accused Moscow of signing the treaty in order to facilitate making war on China.[26] Peking evidently concluded that a question of principle was involved, that the Eastern European countries needed to be reminded of their own real interests, and that it could not remain silent. On September 12, exactly one month after the signing of the treaty, a long interval that undoubtedly reflected uncertainty and perhaps disagreement as to how to react, Peking published a blast against the treaty, which in essence accused Moscow of betraying East German and East European interests; it stopped short, however, of specifically attributing an anti-Chinese purpose to the Soviet Union in this case.[27]

A similar anti-Soviet attitude, obsessive to the point of being countereffective, was reflected in Peking's response to the Polish urban riots of December 1970. On December 22, "Commentator" (an important source) published an article in the People's Daily denouncing both the regime of former First Secretary Gomulka and the Gierek regime that replaced it after the riots for oppressing the Polish working class and the Soviet Union for allegedly threatening armed intervention.[28] Peking's main reward for this pronouncement was a denunciation by Gierek at the time of the Soviet Twenty-fourth Party Congress.[29]

Peking's efforts to normalize its state relations with Eastern Europe, as well as its general campaign of diplomatic normalization, has attracted considerable attention in Eastern Europe. But it appears that, because of Soviet influence and ideological differences and also probably because of occasional clumsy Chinese moves like the one over Poland, the attention to date in the Northern Tier countries (Poland, Czechoslovakia, and East Germany) had been mainly of an unfavorable kind.[30]

---

[26] Radio Tirana broadcast, August 18, 1970.

[27] Text of statement released by New China News Agency, September 12, 1970.

[28] "The Revolutionary Storm of the Polish People," People's Daily, December 22, 1970.

[29] Edward Gierek, "The Immutable Principles of Leninism," Pravda, March 29, 1971.

[30] Cf. j.c.k. (Joseph C. Kun), "China's Changing Relations with Eastern Europe," Radio Free Europe Research Paper, October 13, 1970; j.c.k., "East Europe Wary of Peking's Diplomacy," Radio Free Europe Research Paper, February 18, 1971.

But not in the Balkans. China's relations with Yugoslavia have warmed remarkably since late 1970, and it is highly probable that Peking is trying to do what it can to support Yugoslavia against Soviet pressures which appear to be aimed at the breakup of Yugoslavia after Tito's death.[31] Chinese ideological hostility to Tito, which dates back at least to 1957, is clearly being outweighed by antagonism toward the Soviet Union and a reluctance to see a counterweight to Soviet hegemony over Eastern Europe eliminated or another precedent like the invasion of Czechoslovakia for a possible resumption of direct Soviet pressures on China.

## Ideological and Party Relations

The fact that the current head of the Soviet delegation to the border talks, L. F. Ilyichev, has a background of ideological activity suggests that Moscow is interested in an ideological rapprochement with Peking, on the unlikely supposition that Peking accepts the Soviet position. But, Moscow can hardly entertain much optimism on this score, at least as long as Mao Tse-tung is alive. For Mao's campaign against Soviet "revisionism" seems to have become an indispensable part of his ideological and political outlook and program.

At present the two parties maintain almost no formal relations that might facilitate a compromise. During the months preceding the opening of the Soviet Twenty-fourth Party Congress (March 30-April 9, 1971), Moscow privately explored Peking's attitude toward sending a delegation of observers to the congress. Peking refused, and accordingly no formal invitation was issued.[32]

Mao Tse-tung reminded the world, and especially Moscow, of his opposition to Soviet "revisionism" by means of a major propaganda article published on March 18, the centennial of the Paris Commune.[33] Its impact was reinforced in Peking's eyes by the announcement two days earlier of the successful orbiting of China's second earth satellite (it had actually been launched on March 3); a year before, Peking had timed the launching of its first earth satellite to coincide approximately with the centennial of Lenin's birth, with the issuing of another major anti-Soviet article, and with the holding of the "summit conference of

---

[31] Cf. Dan Morgan in *Washington Post,* June 12, 1971.

[32] Henry S. Hayward in *Christian Science Monitor,* April 10, 1971.

[33] "Long Live the Victory of the Proletariat—in Commemoration of the Centenary of the Paris Commune," *People's Daily, Red Flag,* and *Liberation Army Daily,* March 18, 1971.

the Indochinese peoples." In view of its timing, the March 18, 1971, editorial could also be regarded as an attack on the Soviet Twenty-fourth Congress. Actually, it contained nothing new, except perhaps an even heavier stress than usual for Peking on revolutionary violence: "Violent revolution is the universal principle of proletarian revolution."

Brezhnev made a report to the congress in which he repeated the standard current Soviet version of Sino-Soviet relations: no improvement in ideological and party relations, limited improvement in state relations entirely as a result of Soviet initiatives.[34] This appraisal is essentially correct but it ignores the Soviet pressures on China of 1969 and the fact that ideological and party relations are nearly as frozen on the Soviet side as on the Chinese. Mao Tse-tung's view is that despite "irreconcilable" ideological differences, the Sino-Soviet dispute in the state sphere can be settled "eventually." [35]

## Recent Developments

Given this state of armed truce in Sino-Soviet relations, which was reaffirmed from the Soviet side in a press commentary on the CCP's fiftieth anniversary,[36] Peking has been relatively nonprovocative. For reasons to be indicated later, the main emphasis of its foreign policy is currently directed at the United States, while the Soviet Union is held in a state of uneasy deadlock aided by the Peking talks.

Peking has therefore been reluctant to go beyond limited economic cooperation and warm political generalities in supporting Romania and Yugoslavia, both of which are under severe Soviet pressure and would probably welcome strong Chinese support. Mere contact with these East European states, however, seems to have some value in the eyes of all concerned as an aid in imposing restraint on Moscow.

Romanian President Ceausescu's visit to China (June 1-9, 1971), which was marked by public statements on both sides almost devoid of hostile references to the Soviet Union and containing rather few to the United States, was also marked by signs of disagreement between the two sides. It seems likely that Ceausescu—who may have brought a message to Mao from President Nixon—demanded without success effective support, at least of a declaratory kind, against the Soviet Union;

---

[34] Text in *Pravda*, March 31, 1971.
[35] Edgar Snow, "A Conversation with Mao Tse-tung," *Life*, April 30, 1971, p. 48.
[36] I. Aleksandrov (pseud.), "The Fiftieth Anniversary of the CCP," *Pravda*, July 1, 1971.

what he got instead was the usual Chinese denunciations, vague and not very helpful, of the "two superpowers," the United States and the Soviet Union. It is also likely that the Chinese side was correspondingly unsuccessful in trying to persuade Ceausescu to denounce the United States as strongly as Peking would have liked.[37]

During the period of the Ceausescu visit to China, public Soviet criticism of Peking was muted, as though to avoid pushing it into giving support to the Romanians. Even afterward, emerging Soviet and East European (especially Hungarian) displeasure was aimed more at Romania than at China, and more at Romania's resistance to economic integration within CEMA than at its flirtation with Peking.[38] Peking may have been shielded from Soviet wrath to some extent by its growing contacts with the United States.

The visit to China of Yugoslav Foreign Minister Mirko Tepavac (June 8-15, 1971) was very warmly received. It also was marked by an absence of public attacks on the Soviet Union, and by relative restraint toward the United States. The Yugoslav visit was less sensitive in Moscow's eyes than was the Romanian, since Yugoslavia is not a member of the Warsaw Pact or of CEMA [39] the Council of Mutual Economic Assistance (sometimes known as Comecon).

---

[37] Text of joint communique released by New China News Agency, June 9, 1971. On Sino-Romanian disagreement during the talks see Seymour Topping in *New York Times,* June 9, 1971. Mao's personal message to the Romanian delegation was "Unite and overthrow imperialism and all reactionaries" (New China News Agency dispatch, June 3, 1971); note the lack of reference to "revisionism" or "social imperialism." K'ang Sheng's appearance during the visit may have been intended, in the light of his strong anti-Soviet record (on this point see his biography in Donald W. Klein and Anne B. Clark, *Biographic Dictionary of Chinese Communism,* 2 vols., Harvard University Press, 1971, vol. I, p. 427), to symbolize Peking's determination to maintain the essence of its adversary relationship with Moscow, but K'ang took no part in the actual negotiations with the Romanian delegation.

[38] The economic integration issue as seen from Bucharest is well discussed in Rowland Evans and Robert Novak in *Washington Post,* July 19, 1971. Criticism of Romanian foreign policy, in general terms, by Hungarian Politburo member Zoltan Komocsin (Budapest Domestic Service broadcast, June 24, 1971), was answered in fairly strong language by Romanian Standing Presidium member P. N. Scu-Mizil, "For Strengthening the Friendship and International Solidarity of the Socialist Countries," *Scinteia,* July 9, 1971; for comment see Rowland Evans and Robert Novak in *Washington Post,* July 15, 1971. Romania was not represented at an informal meeting of the CEMA countries held at the beginning of August (see Bernard Gwertzman in *New York Times,* August 3, 1971).

[39] Text of joint communique released by New China News Agency, June 15, 1971.

74

Chinese pronouncements regarding the Soviet Union on the occasion of the 1971 Army Day (August 1) were brief and relatively restrained.[40] By that time Peking had established the form of external contact with the greatest potential utility as a restraint on Moscow, as well as for some other purposes, by receiving Dr. Henry Kissinger (July 9-11) and by extending an invitation to President Nixon to visit China. The Soviet reaction to this spectacular development was unfavorable, but cautiously so, and included an insistence that Moscow was anxious to improve its relations with both the United States and China.[41] A subsequent, authoritative, commentary by the leading Soviet specialist on American affairs displayed somewhat greater concern over the potential effects of growing Sino-American contacts, especially on Soviet-American relations.[42] A detailed, interesting, and apparently authoritative summary of the current Soviet official view of Sino-Soviet relations has recently been given by the Hungarian military analyst Istvan Körmendy, a man with good Soviet contacts:[43]

> ... the signs of a thaw did not give rise to illusions in Moscow even last year. ... They [i.e., Körmendy's Soviet sources] saw as one hidden goal of this modification that Peking was striving to disrupt relations between the Soviet Union and the other socialist countries. ...
>
> Even so, for the Soviet part, they were happy about the thaw and pushing it themselves ... but at one point the Chinese checked the process and repeatedly rejected the Soviet proposals.
>
> A Moscow expert reconstructed the development of the deadlock as follows: The Chinese began to say that they could not talk as an equal partner as long as "the Soviet atom bomb hung over their heads." The Soviets then made a proposal in the form of a short draft treaty, that the two sides renounce

---

[40] Speech by Chief of Staff Huang Yung-sheng, text released by New China News Agency, July 31, 1971; "Commemorate August 1, Army Day," *People's Daily, Red Flag,* and *Liberation Army Daily,* August 1, 1971.

[41] I. Aleksandrov (pseud.), "Regarding Peking-Washington Contacts," *Pravda,* July 25, 1971.

[42] Georgi A. Arbatov, "Questions Calling for a Practical Answer," *Pravda,* August 10, 1971; for excerpts and comment see Bernard Gwertzman in *New York Times,* August 11, 1971. Arbatov is the director of the Institute on the U. S. A. of the Soviet Academy of Sciences.

[43] Istvan Körmendy in *Magyarorszag,* July 25, 1971; for comment see Harry Schwartz in *New York Times,* August 8, 1971. For an analysis of the stalemated border talks from the Chinese point of view, see Neville Maxwell in *Washington Post,* November 13, 1971.

the use of force and the threat of force. When the Chinese side rejected the draft, citing the earlier Soviet-Chinese friendship treaty, the Soviet initiative was that the validity of the treaty be reaffirmed in a joint communique. Again the answer was a rejection, citing formal reasons.

One can infer from this, first of all, that China—despite the statements of the Peking leaders and press—did not make much of the "threat from the north." Had they done so they would have readily accepted the Soviet offer, to which no conditions were attached.

The second inference is that it had become clear that the Chinese leaders were not inclined to sign any treaty or statement which would contradict their assertions concerning the hostile behavior and aggressive desires of the Soviet Union. . . .

In Moscow the rigid and decidedly anti-Soviet behavior of the Chinese is attributed to three causes:

1. It is felt in Peking that the present level of Soviet-Chinese interstate relations is sufficient as a background (with the above-mentioned intent) for further improving their contacts with the European socialist countries.

2. A role is also played in the Chinese conjectures by the idea that an improvement in Soviet-Chinese relations, including closing the border question, would narrow Peking's room for maneuver between the two atomic great powers.

3. Anti-Sovietism is considered a favorable background for carrying out the new Chinese-American rapprochement maneuver.

At present, the most important cause is undoubtedly the third. After the freeze in the further development of Soviet-Chinese contacts, political logic dictated that this would be followed by a thaw between Washington and Peking. For some time Moscow political circles have counted on a gradual Chinese-American rapprochement. They have also noted that despite the rapprochement to come, Chinese-American relations remain fundamentally those of confrontation, but that the improvement in contacts would no doubt have an anti-Soviet edge. . . . News of the [Chinese] invitation [to President Nixon] evoked great surprise, but equally surprising was the observation of a Soviet expert on China, voiced exactly three weeks before the news of the Nixon visit. "Peking is probably interested in aiding the re-election of Nixon in an indirect manner through the improvement of Chinese-American contacts. The coming to power of a Democratic Party regime would be unfavorable to Peking since it might result in better Soviet-American relations." . . . They [i.e., the Chinese] are trying to prove that the United States must settle the Indochinese conflict with China as a partner, and that China has the decisive word in Asian questions.

The central problem for Chinese-American relations is and will be for a time that of Taiwan. . . .

According to the Soviet estimate, a final solution to the Taiwan problem can hardly be expected for a few years. . . . Today every indication points unambiguously to a political solution, especially since the announcement of Nixon's invitation to Peking. . . .

In the opinion of Soviet experts, China will soon have the opportunity to take its place in the world organization [i.e., the United Nations]. . . .

The Soviet side is, in principle, sticking to its position and supports the admission of China, although it realizes that China will hardly make statements favorable to the Soviet Union in the world organization. . . . One does not find any anxiety in Moscow concerning the expected Chinese propaganda campaign. . . .

The Chinese leadership has made especially great efforts to overcome backwardness in the area of the development of rocket-nuclear weapons. . . . For the time being, there are no signs that the possession of nuclear weapons will produce a change in present [Chinese] foreign policy thinking or lead to a fundamental re-evaluation of military doctrine; nor will it cause a change in the balance of power which has developed at the level of strategic nuclear weapons.

The present [Chinese] stocks consist of about 100 to 200 medium range rockets, and it is estimated that by the end of the decade China may have some 150 deployable strategic rockets.

As for the accuracy of this analysis, its general tenor seems reasonable, as a Soviet view at any rate. The generally pessimistic diagnosis and prognosis of China's behavior toward the Soviet Union received additional confirmation when, on August 7, 1971, Peking rejected a Soviet invitation to a five-power nuclear disarmament conference and renewed its own call for a conference of all nations on nuclear disarmament and a no-first-use agreement among the three major nuclear powers.[44]

Following the announcement in mid-July 1971 that President Nixon would visit China by May 1972, the Soviet press was filled to an even greater extent than usual with denunciations of Peking. The charges,

---

[44] *New York Times,* August 8, 1971.

invariably exaggerated and sometimes false, included old ones such as the myth that Peking had a "military psychosis" and was trying to dominate the world through involving the United States and the Soviet Union in general war with each other,[45] and new ones like the accusation that Washington and Peking had made a secret agreement on economic cooperation.[46] An eminent Soviet China specialist, taking a more conciliatory line, distorted the past by denying that the Soviet Union had ever given China any genuine reason for fearing a Soviet attack.[47] This propaganda barrage probably reflected the Soviet leadership's concern not only over the trend toward improvement in Sino-American relations but over the lack of progress in the Peking border talks, Chinese political gains in Eastern Europe, and growing public apathy in the Soviet Union toward official efforts to exploit the China issue for political effect.

Peking replied to the Soviet charges only rarely, and on specific points, apart from accusing Moscow of betraying East Germany by signing an agreement on West Berlin with the Western Allies.[48] This comparative Chinese reticence is consistent with the view advanced in this study that China has been avoiding unnecessary provocation of Moscow while improving its relations with other powers, especially the United States, partly as political insurance against the possibility that the Soviet Union might resort once more to military pressure to impose its will on China.

### The Future of Sino-Soviet Relations

It seems plausible to expect a continuation of the current trend toward partial normalization of the Sino-Soviet relationship in the state field, including economic relations. There is likely, however, to be at least one major exception to this generalization, namely the border issue. This involves, not only actual territory, always a sensitive question, but strong feelings. The Chinese for their part undoubtedly resent the Soviet per-

---

[45] I. Aleksandrov (pseud.), "The Slogans and Deeds of the Chinese Leadership," *Pravda,* September 4, 1971 (for comment see Bernard Gwertzman in *New York Times,* September 4, 1971). See also S. Yurkov, "An Unwise Policy," *Izvestia,* August 26, 1971 (for comment see Bernard Gwertzman in *New York Times,* August 26, 1971).

[46] Tass dispatch, September 6, 1971.

[47] S. L. Tikhvinsky, "Soviet-Chinese Relations: Supporters and Opponents of Their Improvement," *Pravda,* August 20, 1971 (for comment see Bernard Gwertzman in *New York Times,* August 21, 1971).

[48] New China News Agency dispatch, September 9, 1971 (for comment see Tillman Durdin in *New York Times,* September 10, 1971).

formance in 1969 and fear and distrust Moscow accordingly, much as they feared the pressures exerted by the United States on China in the 1950s. For the sake of face at home and abroad, Peking is likely to continue demanding concessions, including an admission of the "unequal" border treaties, that Moscow will find it hard to make; the same is true of the demands that Peking will make for major concessions on Taiwan as the minimum price for an accommodation with the United States.

As for the Soviet side, it has been suggested that once the Federal Republic of Germany normalizes its relations with the Soviet Union and accepts the Oder-Neisse line—which will presumably be accomplished by ratification of the 1970 treaties with the Soviet Union and Poland in exchange for some concessions on West Berlin—the entire territorial question might lose some of its sensitivity in Moscow's eyes and some territorial concessions might be forthcoming to China and possibly Japan.[49] It might be argued at least as persuasively that, since Bonn has no choice but to accept, sooner or later, the essentials of the status quo in Central Europe, once it does so Moscow will feel more strongly than ever that there is no reason to offer Peking, and perhaps Tokyo, anything more favorable than the status quo with respect to the Far East. An obvious possible tactic, before or after a settlement with West Germany, would be for Moscow to give Japan the relatively unimportant islands it wants so as to minimize the chances of a Sino-Japanese combination against the Soviet Union, at least on the territorial issue. However, since Sino-Japanese relations are basically hostile it is doubtful whether Moscow would see any need for such a settlement. In short, the outlook is probably for continued wrangling on the Sino-Soviet border issue for some time—at least until there has been a change of leadership on one or both sides.

On the other hand, Peking and Moscow are not likely to go to war, although isolated clashes are always a possibility in spite of the quiet that has generally prevailed since September 1969. The disincentives to war are very powerful on both sides. The writer finds it impossible to develop this point any better than he has in a previous work: [50]

> . . . one cannot doubt that Chinese leaders recognize the exist-
> ence of powerful disincentives to any major war with the Soviet
> Union, whether over territorial boundaries or anything else.

---

[49] R. Waring Herrick, "Soviet Far East Policies Hamstrung by Fear of Irredentism," *Radio Liberty Dispatch,* March 23, 1971.
[50] Harold C. Hinton, "Conflict on the Ussuri: A Clash of Nationalisms," *Problems of Communism,* vol. xx, nos. 1-2 (January-April 1971), pp. 58-59.

In addition to the obviously great superiority of the Soviet Union in military-industrial strength and strategic weapons, the Chinese realize that they would face serious logistical difficulties in any Sino-Soviet conflict, as well as the risk of renewed political discord at home. . . .

On the Soviet side, too, there are powerful disincentives to war. From the military standpoint, major Soviet offensive operations on Chinese soil not only could be expected to encounter numerically superior Chinese forces in most areas, and probably a militantly hostile populace, but also would entail serious logistical problems. China's defensive preparations, moreover, have been extensive, reportedly including the reorganization for military purposes of the sprawling Inner Mongolia Autonomous Region so as to place most of it under the Mukden, Peking, and Lanchow Military Regions, thereby improving the possibilities for a coordinated defense in depth.

The political deterrents are as cogent as the military. To begin with, there is no persuasive evidence to indicate that Moscow would be capable of establishing or calling into being any Chinese collaborationist regime, except perhaps on a localized scale in border regions with large non-Chinese populations. Such being the case, for the Soviet Union to attempt a Czechoslovakia-type military intervention in China to enforce the Brezhnev Doctrine would, in all probability, be futile; and more than that, the end result would be to intensify traditional Chinese hatred of the Russians and thus to render illusory any Soviet hopes of reestablishing the unity of the Communist world under Moscow's leadership.

In addition to these arguments, the "doves" in Moscow—who are believed to include some highly placed military figures—can point to still other considerations supporting their position. Among these are China's recently enhanced political standing in Asia, the inadvisability of driving China and the United States together, the probable alienation of foreign Communist parties if the Soviet Union were to go to war with China, and the need to give higher priority to the solution of persistent economic problems at home as well as to the protection and strengthening of the Soviet position in Europe and the Middle East.

The possibility must be admitted, however, that the Soviet Union might assume that Mao's death would be followed by serious leadership conflict and popular demoralization, and therefore might give serious consideration to applying pressure, presumably short of actual war, at that time with the aim of inducing political concessions. The probability of such an attempt is impossible to predict.

As for the chances of a Sino-Soviet rapprochement, it is conceivable that common fear of Japan might produce a resurrection of the Sino-Soviet alliance, but not unless Japan builds its armed forces to offensive levels; this, in spite of much Soviet and Chinese propaganda to the contrary, Japan has no present plans to do. In the party-ideological field, a rapprochement appears improbable at least as long as Mao Tse-tung, Brezhnev (party), and Suslov (ideological) all remain active. There is certainly no current evidence of a trend toward such a rapprochement. It is entirely possible that in time the ideological (although probably not the party) component of each side's thinking and behavior will decline in importance to a point where, if there is no real rapprochement, neither is there a real dispute.

On the whole, as an eminent authority has recently written, "The continuation of limited and controlled conflict between Russia and China thus remains a far more plausible prospect than its end by either reunion or catastrophe." [51]

> On the other hand [as the present writer has pointed out] [52] there are some factors that might, under certain conditions, become powerful enough to swing the balance in Moscow in favor of stepped-up military pressure, or possibly even a major attack, on China. For one thing, the nature and scope of the Soviet military buildup in Asia are such as to suggest that Moscow is determined to command a full range of conventional and nuclear options, up to and including a nuclear first-strike capability, whether preemptive or as the prelude to an all-out attack. Obviously, the availability of these options tends to create, under conditions of tension, the temptation to use one or another of them.
>
> Meanwhile, there is little question that Peking, by dragging its feet in the border negotiations and in the matter of normalizing Sino-Soviet intergovernmental relations, and by continuing to display uncompromising political and ideological hostility toward Moscow, is sorely taxing the patience of the Soviet leaders and tempting them to bring increased military pressure on China in order to force a retreat. Also, the recent trend toward improved Soviet relations with the West—evidenced by the SALT talks, the Soviet treaty with West Germany, the Middle East truce, and the absence of a Soviet-US confrontation over Cambodia—tends to ease Moscow's fear

[51] Richard Lowenthal, "Russia and China: Controlled Conflict," *Foreign Affairs,* vol. 49, no. 3 (April 1971), p. 518.
[52] Hinton, "Conflict on the Ussuri: A Clash of Nationalisms," *op. cit.,* p. 59.

of a two-front war and thus to heighten the temptation to teach China a lesson while conditions are favorable. Given, in addition to all this, Moscow's long-range fear of a historically hostile China which is well along the road to acquiring a thermonuclear force capable of striking the Soviet Union, the temptation to launch a preemptive attack—rationalized, of course, as a defensive measure—must be considerable. It may be partly with this eventuality in mind that Moscow has been endeavoring to broaden the scope of its alliance system in Eastern Europe to cover an attack by "any state or group of states."

In short, the possible courses that Sino-Soviet relations may take in the foreseeable future cover the full spectrum of alternatives, ranging from peace to war—including, of course, the classic Communist condition of neither war nor peace.

# 5

## The United States and the Sino-Soviet Dispute

It has become a commonplace to say that the Sino-Soviet dispute has expanded the pattern of great power interrelationships into a triangle, which may soon become a quadrilateral by virtue of the growing importance of Japan. This study focuses its attention on certain aspects of the Sino-Soviet relationship and does not pretend to explore in depth any of the other relationships among the parties to this triangle or quadrilateral. The present chapter therefore emphasizes, as its title indicates, the American aspect of the Sino-Soviet dispute without attempting to deal with the broader subjects of American policy toward China or the Soviet Union, except to the extent that the analysis of the principal subject seems to require.

### Historical Background

At the time the Chinese Communists came to power, there was little reason for the United States to assume that the Chinese relationship with the Soviet Union was anything but what Peking said it was, namely "monolithic." Mao Tse-tung had asserted in mid-1949 that his regime would "lean to one side," toward the Soviet Union in its Cold War with the United States;[1] and in early 1950 he signed with Stalin a mili-

---

[1] "On the People's Democratic Dictatorship" (June 30, 1949), in *Selected Works of Mao Tse-tung,* Peking: Foreign Languages Press, vol. iv, 1961, p. 415. In 1944-1946 the CCP had given tentative indications of interest in friendly relations with the United States as a means of counterbalancing the Soviet Union and discouraging American support for the Nationalists in the Chinese civil war, but American commitments to the Nationalists as the recognized government prevented reciprocation of these overtures, and by 1949 the intervening period of civil war, in which the United States had supported the losing side, and the growing (although by no means total) closeness between the CCP and the Soviet

tary alliance against Japan or "any other state which should unite with Japan, directly or indirectly, in acts of aggression," meaning obviously the United States.[2] Any hope in Washington that in the longer term China would reject the Stalinist domination to which it seemed likely to be subjected [3] was crushed soon afterward by the outbreak of the Korean War in June 1950 and by Chinese intervention in the war, seemingly in close coordination with the Soviet Union if not on Soviet orders.[4] United States antagonism to Communist China and a conviction of its subservience to the Soviet Union were industriously fanned in the public mind by a powerful "China Lobby," including influential "Formosa Firsters" in Congress.[5]

During this period General MacArthur was almost alone in stating that the Sino-Soviet relationship was less than "monolithic"; he believed that the Soviet Union was most unlikely to intervene militarily in the Far East in response to the employment of American air and sea power against China, which he was recommending.[6] On the other hand, the Truman administration's official position was that the Soviet Union might very well respond to American escalation against China by intervening in the Far East by attacking Western Europe.[7] The official position of

---

Union rendered the question obsolete. For comments on the 1944-1946 interlude see John S. Service, *The Amerasia Papers: Some Problems in the History of US-China Relations,* University of California: Center for Chinese Studies, 1971, pp. 176-183; testimony of Allen S. Whiting before the Senate Foreign Relations Committee, June 25, 1971.

[2] Sino-Soviet treaty of February 14, 1950, Article I.

[3] Cf. Dean Acheson, letter of transmittal to the China White Paper (*United States Relations With China With Special Reference to the Period 1944-1949,* Washington: Department of State, August 1949, pp. xvi-xvii); Dean Acheson, speech of January 12, 1950 (text in *China and U.S. Far East Policy, 1945-1966,* Washington: Congressional Quarterly Service, 1967, pp. 257-261).

[4] Cf. speech of May 18, 1951, by Assistant Secretary of State Dean Rusk (text in *Miiltary Situation in the Far East,* Washington, U.S. Government Printing Office, 1951, vol. 5, pp. 3190-3192).

[5] For an objective brief description of groups in the United States on both sides of the question then attempting to influence policy and public opinion, see *China and U.S. Far East Policy, 1945-1966,* Washington: Congressional Quarterly Service, 1967, pp. 23-28.

[6] *Military Situation in the Far East,* vol. 1, p. 6.

[7] The Acheson memoirs (Dean Acheson, *Present at the Creation: My Years in the State Department,* New York: Norton, 1969) are not clear on this point, which however is implicit in General Bradley's famous phrase that a major war with China would be the "wrong war, at the wrong place, at the wrong time, and with the wrong enemy" (*Military Situation in the Far East,* vol. 2, p. 732) and was clearly stated by General Marshall in his testimony following the relief of General MacArthur (*ibid.,* vol. 1, p. 325). See also David Rees, *Korea: The Limited War,* New York: St. Martin's Press, 1964, p. 281.

course prevailed, at least until the Eisenhower administration saw fit, in February-March 1953, to threaten Peking with nuclear weapons as a means of compelling it to agree to an armistice.[8] This threat found the Soviet Union, then plunged into confusion on account of Stalin's death and the ensuing succession crisis, unable and unwilling to render China effective support, and the result may well have been the most serious strain to which the Sino-Soviet relationship had been subjected up to that time.[9]

Whatever Sino-Soviet tensions may have existed at that time were insufficiently understood on the outside, however, to disturb the official American view that Sino-Soviet relations were essentially "monolithic." This continued to be Washington's appreciation even though there were signs of friction and lack of coordination between Peking and Moscow at the time of the Geneva Conference of 1954 [10] and the East European crisis of 1956.[11] By about 1958, it was becoming clear to sophisticated Western analysts, but not yet to American policymakers, that the Twentieth Congress of the CPSU (February 1956), and particularly Khrushchev's attack on Stalin, had inaugurated a period of serious tension in Sino-Soviet relations.[12] Even during the Peking-initiated military crisis of 1958 in the Taiwan Strait, which to the analyst reveals clear signs of Sino-Soviet conflicts of interest,[13] the official American view was that Peking and Moscow were acting in unison. Obviously a dispute whose existence was not recognized at the highest level in the United States could not be consciously exploited, regardless of whether objective opportunities to do so existed.

It was only after the important Moscow Conference of November-December 1960, at which Sino-Soviet differences were vigorously aired

---

[8] Reed, op. cit., Chapter 22.

[9] Harold C. Hinton, Communist China in World Politics, Boston: Houghton Mifflin, 1966, pp. 222-229.

[10] Harrison E. Salisbury, War Between Russia and China, New York: Bantam, 1970, pp. 85-87.

[11] Donald S. Zagoria, The Sino-Soviet Conflict, 1956-1961, Princeton University Press, 1962, pp. 54-65.

[12] The official Chinese version of this deterioration is given in "The Origin and Development of the Differences Between the Leadership of the CPSU and Ourselves," People's Daily and Red Flag, September 6, 1963 (text in The Polemic on the General Line of the International Communist Movement, Peking: Foreign Languages Press, 1965, pp. 57-114).

[13] Zagoria, op. cit., Chapter 7; John R. Thomas, "The Quemoy Crisis of 1958," in Raymond L. Garthoff, ed., Sino-Soviet Military Relations, New York: Frederick A. Praeger, 1966, Chapter 7.

before frequently astounded delegates from other Communist parties,[14] that American policymakers began fully to understand that there existed a Sino-Soviet dispute that was serious and not merely a "nonantagonistic contradiction" which could be resolved within the framework of the Marxist dialectic. It was now clearly perceived by nearly everyone that there were at least two major issues under debate between Peking and Moscow: the best method of coping with American "imperialism," and the best strategy for promoting and supporting the "national liberation movement" in the Third World.[15] On these issues the Chinese were the more militant or "dogmatist," the Russians the more moderate or "revisionist." Soon it was perceived that the differences were so great, and the Chinese conduct of the dispute so vigorous, as to indicate a challenge by Peking to Moscow's organizational and ideological leadership of the international Communist movement with the apparent aim of setting itself up insofar as possible not only as a rival but as a successor.[16] It was less widely understood—at least before Peking began to publicize its grievances in 1963, after the signing of the nuclear test ban treaty— that there were serious differences of national as well as ideological interest between China and the Soviet Union. These included, for example, policy toward India and the question of the Sino-Indian border dispute, into which it is not necessary to go here. But there was one major Sino-Soviet conflict of national interest that does need to be discussed, because it relates directly to the United States: the one over the Sino-American military confrontation along China's eastern periphery, centering on but not confined to Taiwan.

The United States and the Soviet Union, from the time of the outbreak of the Korean War, regardless of the state of the strategic balance between them and their willingness to engage in occasional mutual confrontations in Europe and over the Middle East, were eager to avoid confrontation over the Far East. Both sides seemed to believe that such a confrontation might lead to the "wrong war, at the wrong place, at the

---

[14] The first authoritative public discussion of the conference and its background from this viewpoint was Edward Crankshaw in *Washington Post,* February 12, 1961. For a fuller account see William E. Griffith, "The November 1960 Moscow Meeting: A Preliminary Reconstruction," *The China Quarterly,* no. 11 (July-September 1962), pp. 38-57.

[15] Allen S. Whiting, "Moscow and Peking: Suspended Dialogue?" *Current Scene* (Hong Kong), vol. i, no. 4 (June 21, 1961).

[16] Cf. William E. Griffith, *Albania and the Sino-Soviet Rift,* M.I.T. Press, 1963, pp. 37, 89.

wrong time," even if not with the "wrong enemy." Under these circumstances the Soviet Union felt unable to give China any more direct support in its recurrent crises with the United States than military aid and a limited amount of diplomatic and propaganda support. This was essentially true during the Korean War. Khrushchev gave Peking no declaratory support at the time of the Taiwan Strait crisis of 1954-55, even though the crisis began at about the time of his first visit to China. His declaratory support for Peking during the Taiwan Strait crisis of 1958 was timed so as to come when the risk of escalation had begun to recede.[17] Five years later Peking publicly ridiculed his performance.[18] Khrushchev's refusal to do more for China against the United States, especially at a time when Peking was insisting that "The East wind has prevailed over the West wind" and that Moscow was the "head" of the international Communist movement, must have contrasted sharply in Chinese eyes with his "ultimatum" to the West over Berlin, issued on November 10, 1958, after the Taiwan Strait crisis was safely over and he was therefore not risking two crises with the United States at once. If, on the other hand, Khrushchev had delivered his Berlin "ultimatum" during the Taiwan Strait crisis, Peking might have benefited considerably from the diversionary effect.

It was probably on account of Peking's disgust with Khrushchev's performance at that time that a collection of Mao Tse-tung's past statements in praise of the Soviet Union,[19] published in November 1958 apparently as a companion piece to the famous anti-American collection on the "paper tiger" theme, was given almost no publicity after publication. At the end of September 1959 Khrushchev, fresh from his friendly trip to the United States, rubbed salt in what the Chinese regarded as their wounds by advising them, during a visit to Peking, to tolerate indefinitely the existence of a separate Taiwan, as a contribution to the peace and stability of Asia.[20]

It is reasonably clear, then, that the United States made a major contribution to the Sino-Soviet dispute by denying Taiwan to Peking, engaging in war with Peking in Korea and in confrontation with it over

---

[17] Thomas, *loc. cit.*

[18] Chinese government statement, September 1, 1963 (text in Garthoff, *op. cit.,* pp. 222-238; see p. 233).

[19] "Chairman Mao on the October Revolution," *Hsin Hua Pan-yueh-k'an* (New China Fortnightly), no. 22 (November 1958), pp. 1-8.

[20] See note 18.

Indochina and thus indirectly revealing to Peking the limited extent to which it could realistically count on Soviet support in such situations. What is involved here is a matter of historical interpretation, not implicit praise or blame for United States policy.

Under the Kennedy administration there was a greater reluctance than under President Eisenhower to engage in confrontation with either the Soviet Union or China; the main exception was the Cuban missile crisis of 1963 which involved the Soviet Union, not China. Virtually ignoring the various small olive branches extended in its direction by the United States after 1961, Peking vigorously denounced the simultaneous American gestures to the Soviet Union and Khrushchev's occasional responses to them, notably the nuclear test ban treaty, as evidence of Soviet-American "collusion" to "encircle" China and indeed to dominate the world.[21] The test ban and other later arms control agreements involving the United States and the Soviet Union, far from moving Peking to join them, have only increased its suspicion of "collusion" with the purpose of frustrating China's ambition to become a nuclear power.

The replacement of Khrushchev in October 1964 by a new Soviet leadership under Brezhnev and Kosygin, almost as anti-Chinese as he and more anti-American, made no alterations in the relationship of the United States to the Sino-Soviet dispute. The escalation of the war in Vietnam in early 1965, however, did so to a limited extent. A new issue, that of "united action" by the Communist states on behalf of Hanoi, was piled on those already dividing Peking from Moscow. More important from the American point of view was the widespread feeling in the United States of being embarked on a "collision course" with China on account of Vietnam; this led to the adoption in 1966 of a more conciliatory American tone, usually described with the slogan, "containment without isolation," [22] toward Peking, and to some sort of informal and unpublished understanding with Peking, apparently

[21] Cf. the reference to the "vain pursuit of world domination through U.S.-Soviet collaboration" in "Peaceful Coexistence—Two Diametrically Opposed Policies," *People's Daily* and *Red Flag*, December 12, 1963 (text in *The Polemic. . . , op. cit.*, p. 355).

[22] This expression gained currency at the time of the Senate Foreign Relations Committee hearings on China in March 1966 (*U.S. Policy with Respect to Mainland China*, Washington: U.S. Government Printing Office, 1966); see also statement by Secretary of State Dean Rusk during the same hearings (text in *New York Times*, April 17, 1966).

reached at Warsaw in mid-March 1966, to the effect that neither would attack the other as long as the Vietnam war was not further escalated by the other.[23] These developments gave rise to exaggerated concern in Moscow that the United States and China might be beginning to cooperate in some way that would be adverse to Soviet interests. Soviet apprehension on this score has continued to exist to the present time.[24] At least until the dramatic improvement in Sino-American relations that occurred in 1971, however, Moscow apparently did not consider the prospects of a Sino-American rapprochement to be great enough to require a Soviet effort at a rapprochement with either China or the United States.

But Soviet concern over Sino-American relations tended to be outweighed, after early 1966, by concern over the Cultural Revolution. For the first time, Moscow began to give Peking serious reason to fear Soviet military action against it, by reinforcing the Soviet military presence in Mongolia, for example. Even so, Peking felt unable to move closer to the United States on account of Chinese objections to American involvement in the Vietnam war, Chinese reservations about the Paris negotiations between the United States and North Vietnam, the continuing problem of Taiwan, and the hostility of American "imperialism" which is central to the "thought" of Mao Tse-tung. It was only after the invasion of Czechoslovakia that Mao gave signs of being sufficiently concerned over the Soviet threat to favor some improvement of relations with Western countries, apparently including the United States.[25] Even so, the militant political atmosphere of the months preceding the Ninth Party Congress led to the cancellation of the Sino-American ambassadorial meeting scheduled for February 20, 1969; it also prevented anything positive from being done to improve relations with other Western countries until after the congress, apart from the opening of the talks with Canada in January 1969.

## The Nixon Administration and the Sino-Soviet Dispute

In a series of authoritative public statements,[26] the Nixon administration

[23] Max Frankel in *New York Times,* January 17, 1967.
[24] Cf. Christian Duevel, "Some Thoughts on Soviet-American Relations: An Overview," *Radio Liberty Dispatch,* June 26, 1969.
[25] See Chapter 2.
[26] Richard Nixon, *U.S. Foreign Policy for the 1970's: A New Strategy for Peace,* Washington: U.S. Government Printing Office, February 1970, p. 142; *United*

has insisted that it desires better relations with both the Soviet Union and China and will not be deterred from improving its relations with either by possible objections on the part of the third party. As for the Sino-Soviet dispute, the Nixon administration has asserted that it sees no advantage for the United States in the dispute and will not try to exploit it in any way, let alone take sides in it. The rationale for this position appears to be that exploitation of the dispute by the United States is a virtual impossibility; and even if it were possible, any exploitation might tend either to push them together or produce war between them; in any case it would complicate the relations of the United States with both countries.

The public position of the United States, while not necessarily deceptive, does not provide a full explanation of the policy actually pursued. President Nixon not only is keenly aware of the Soviet Union's power but seems to retain a negative attitude toward it dating from at least as far back as his famous Kitchen Debate of 1959 with Khrushchev in Moscow over a variety of Soviet-American issues. His administration has felt serious concern over the growth of the Soviet Union's strategic military capability, its failure to play a constructive role in promoting a political settlement in Vietnam, and its adventuristic policy in the Middle East.[27] It was for roughly these reasons that the President told news commentator Howard K. Smith, on July 1, 1970, that he favored an improvement of relations with China, and he added that the tension on the Sino-Soviet border constituted a "weakness" in the Soviet position.[28] The rationale of the Nixon administration's policy of trying to achieve a piecemeal improvement of its relations with China, however, is considerably more complex than a desire to gain leverage on the Soviet Union; in view of the public interest that this policy has aroused it may be useful to elaborate on what the writer understands that rationale to be.

The Johnson administration operated, at least until late 1967 or early 1968, on the assumption that the American economy and American

*States Foreign Policy, 1969-1970: A Report of the Secretary of State,* Washington: Department of State Publication 8575, March 1971, p. 44; Secretary Rogers, speeches or press conferences of April 7, 1969 (*Major Public Statements on China by U.S. Officials* [1969-1970], Washington: U.S. Information Agency, January 1971, p. 7); August 8, 1969 (*ibid.,* p. 20); December 23, 1969 (*ibid.,* p. 34); January 15, 1970 (*ibid.,* p. 42). Speech by Under Secretary of State Elliot L. Richardson, September 5, 1969 (*ibid.,* p. 22). Speech by Assistant Secretary of State Marshall Green, January 28, 1970 (*ibid.,* p. 49).

[27] Cf. *U.S. Foreign Policy for the 1970's,* pp. 137-138.

[28] United Press International dispatch, *Washington Post,* July 11, 1970.

public opinion would bear whatever burden might be imposed by the administration's perception of what needed to be done about Vietnam. American policy toward Vietnam had as one of its costs the fact that that policy contributed heavily to rendering out of the question any significant progress toward better relations with Peking. The psychological impact of the North Vietnamese Tet offensive of 1968 completed the process of making the governing assumption false, or at least obsolete.

President Nixon came into office committed in effect to a major inversion of priorities. The restoration of tranquillity at home would be the main objective, and Asia would have to take second place.[29] The Nixon Doctrine, which was announced in July 1969, clearly foreshadowed a large-scale reduction of the American military presence in Asia, especially Vietnam.[30] Hopefully Japan, whose central importance in the region had already been recognized by the President [31] would play a role of "partnership" with the United States and would constructively fill whatever vacuum might be created by a lowering of the American profile.[32] As Assistant Secretary of State for East Asian and Pacific Affairs the President appointed Marshall Green, an experienced career diplomat with a Japanese orientation and a strong commitment to a lower American profile and a more flexible policy toward China. Green appears, in fact, to be the intellectual father of the Nixon Doctrine, or at least of its central assumption to the effect that Asian countries can and should cope with their own internal security problems without direct American involvement. The views on this subject of Henry Kissinger, the President's Assistant for National Security Affairs, were less clear; in an important essay [33] published shortly before taking office, he had not expressed any opinion on policy toward China or the Sino-Soviet dispute.

From the time of his inauguration, the President was apparently determined to improve relations with China, in spite of the discouraging beginning represented by Peking's cancellation of the ambassadorial

29 Cf. Richard M. Nixon, "Asia After Viet Nam," *Foreign Affairs,* vol. 46, no. 1 (October 1967), pp. 113-114.

30 For an authoritative interpretation of the doctrine see *United States Foreign Policy, 1969-1970,* pp. 36-39.

31 Nixon, *loc. cit.,* pp. 120-121.

32 *U.S. Foreign Policy for the 1970's,* pp. 57-58.

33 Henry A. Kissinger, "Central Issues of American Foreign Policy," in Kermit Gordon ed., *Agenda for the Nation,* Washington: Brookings Institution, 1968, pp. 585-614.

meeting scheduled for February 20, 1969. By mid-1969 the time seemed ripe for a fresh U.S. approach to China. The Cultural Revolution and the Ninth Party Congress were over, and the essence of Peking's policy appeared to be stabilization at home and normalization of diplomatic relations at least to the pre-Cultural Revolution level. Canada had recently begun negotiations for diplomatic relations with Peking. An additional element of flexibility was a series of informal contacts between the Soviet Union and Nationalist China. Most important of all, China was under Soviet politico-military pressure on account of the Sino-Soviet border dispute, and it was probably hoped in Washington that Peking would therefore be more flexible in its attitude toward the United States and conceivably toward Taiwan. A desire not to lose any potentially beneficial side effects of Soviet pressure on China may have been a reason why the Nixon administration did not give Peking even verbal support of the kind that President Johnson had given Romania (but not Czechoslovakia) when it was under Soviet pressure a year earlier, by exhorting Moscow not to attack Romania.

In July 1969 a limited relaxation of the American restrictions on trade with and travel to the mainland of China was announced. It was presumably hoped that this step, and similar ones that followed during the next year,[34] would create a better climate in Sino-American relations, facilitate American disengagement from Asia, and perhaps enlist Peking's cooperation, which was said to be essential,[35] in a political settlement for Vietnam. Another consideration behind the more flexible policy toward China, as already mentioned, was a hope of getting into a better position to cope with the Soviet Union, which was known to be extraordinarily sensitive to any hint of improvement in Sino-American relations. There was little reason to expect a major domestic backlash against a more flexible China policy, and in fact there was a growing enthusiasm on the part of American business for the idea of trading with mainland China.[36]

Given these conditions and considerations, it seemingly made sense for the United States to cultivate Peking's supposed greater flexibility by modifying existing American policy toward China and by making more significant changes in policy toward Indochina. It does not appear that in 1969 a serious interest existed on the administration's part in moving

---

[34] *United States Foreign Policy, 1969-1970,* pp. 42-43.
[35] Secretary Rogers once called China "the key to the future of Indochina" (interview of July 8, 1970, in *Major Public Statements on China,* p. 63).
[36] Brendan Jones in *New York Times,* April 18, 1971.

toward a two China (or one China, one Taiwan) policy, either in the United Nations or in any other respect.

A standing invitation had long been out to Peking to resume the Sino-American ambassadorial talks at Warsaw, which had been suspended since early 1968. When Peking, after attending two sessions of the talks in January and February 1970, canceled another session scheduled for May 20 because of American intervention in Cambodia, the Nixon administration had one more reason for exercising greater caution in the future about making even temporary exceptions, as it had by invading Cambodia, to the general trend toward American disengagement from Indochina.

It has recently become publicly known that the Nixon administration tried after the withdrawal of American ground forces at the end of June 1970, to compensate for the interruption of the talks and to convince Peking of the sincerity of its desire for better Sino-American relations by sending private messages through a variety of intermediaries from third countries.[37] A major reappraisal of China policy was evidently undertaken in Washington following the Sino-Canadian agreement of October 1970 on the establishment of diplomatic relations. The urgency of the problem was underlined in November by the majority vote in the United Nations General Assembly in favor of the Albanian resolution, which as in previous years called for the expulsion of Taipei and the seating of Peking, even though the vote did not take effect because of the prior passage of the American-sponsored "important question" resolution requiring a two-thirds majority in the General Assembly before the Chinese seat could be transferred.

At the end of 1970, American official statements seemed to suggest that the policy reappraisal had settled on a two Chinas (or one China, one Taiwan) policy in the United Nations at any rate; in effect, the United States would now concentrate on trying to keep Taipei in the United Nations rather than on trying to keep Peking out.[38] Presumably it was hoped that this could somehow be made acceptable to Peking, as well as Taipei. In the administration's "state of the world" message published in February 1971, mainland China was not only referred to by its official title, the People's Republic of China, but was discussed

---

[37] Edgar Snow, "A Conversation with Mao Tse-tung," *Life*, April 30, 1971, p. 47.

[38] Cf. Murrey Marder in *Washington Post*, November 6, 1970; James M. Naughton in *New York Times*, November 14, 1970.

ahead of the (Nationalist) Republic of China.[39] The decision not to send American ground forces into Laos (in February-March 1971) had the effect, and probably the purpose, among other things, of minimizing the chances of Chinese counterinvolvement and the damage to the prospects for improvement in Sino-American relations.

In mid-March the administration took the important step of removing all remaining restrictions on travel by American citizens to mainland China,[40] and it was announced a month later that a further, although still limited, relaxation of trade restrictions would be put into effect.[41] Moscow was assured at that time by White House Press Secretary Ronald Ziegler that these moves were not designed to put pressure on the Soviet Union.[42] Late in April, the Lodge Commission reported to the President in favor of a two Chinas solution in the United Nations, but within a broader framework of universal representation for all de facto states.[43] At about the same time, in what appears to have been a display of bureaucratic confusion, State Department spokesman Charles Bray suggested talks between Peking and Taipei on the status of Taiwan, which the United States officially considers to be "undetermined." [44] The negative response from both Peking [45] and Taipei [46] was thought by some to have convinced remaining doubters in Washington that a two Chinas policy in any simple form was unworkable, at least in the near future.[47] On June 10, a fairly extensive list of goods and products now exportable to China without a license was announced, and all restrictions on imports from China were removed.[48] The list, however, was not so extensive as that of goods permitted to be exported to the Soviet Union.

For many years Peking's major public demands on the United States have been reasonably constant. Essentially, they have been that the

[39] United States Foreign Policy, 1969-1970, pp. 42-46.

[40] Ted Szulc in New York Times, March 16, 1971.

[41] Robert B. Semple, Jr., in New York Times, April 15, 1971.

[42] Terence Smith in New York Times, April 16, 1971.

[43] Report of the President's Commission for the Observance of the Twenty-Fifth Anniversary of the United Nations, Washington: U.S. Government Printing Office, 1971, pp. 34-37.

[44] Chalmers Roberts in Washington Post, April 29, 1971.

[45] Commentator, "New Evidence of Crimes and the U.S. Government's Hostility Toward the Chinese People," People's Daily, May 4, 1971.

[46] New York Times, May 1, 1971.

[47] Cf. Tad Szulc in New York Times, May 11, 1971.

[48] New York Times, June 11, 1971.

United States give up its alleged objective of "two Chinas"; recognize that Taiwan is Chinese (and not of "undetermined" status); withdraw American forces from the Taiwan area; and observe the principle of "peaceful coexistence" in its behavior toward China (which at the minimum would rule out American interference with Peking's "liberation" of Taiwan).[49]

At first Peking claimed to be concerned over the Nixon administration's alleged desire to "collude with Soviet revisionism," to the disadvantage of China and others.[50] However, it soon began to show a more sophisticated attitude. In the atmosphere of diplomatic normalization following the Ninth Party Congress, Peking noticeably refrained from denouncing those gestures that the United States had begun to make toward China after mid-1969. The reasons for this self-restraint were probably two: Peking was worried by the Soviet threat and hopeful of some sort of effective American support in that connection; also Peking was impressed by the apparent earnestness of President Nixon's determination to wind down American military involvement in Indochina and in fact in the Western Pacific. Beginning in November 1969, the Nixon-Sato communique and the subsequent adoption of a more "self-reliant" defense policy by Japan raised fears in Peking of American collusion with a rearming Japan.[51] Nevertheless, as we have seen, Peking was sufficiently worried by the possibility of the collapse of the border talks with the Soviet Union so that it agreed to ambassadorial talks with the United States on January 20 and February 20, 1970. Even after the cancellation of the session scheduled for May 20, Peking kept some lines open to the United States by indicating an interest in resuming the ambassadorial talks at some more favorable time. Also, once American ground forces had been withdrawn from Cambodia, Peking released Bishop James Walsh from his prolonged imprisonment (in July) and admitted the journalist Edgar Snow (in August) for what turned out to be a six-month visit.

---

[49] Cf. Chou En-lai's remarks quoted in Edgar Snow, *The Other Side of the River: Red China Today*, New York: Random House, 1961, pp. 91-92.

[50] "Nixon Reiterates Counter-Revolutionary Policy of Stepping Up Global Collusion with Soviet Revisionism," New China News Agency dispatch, February 8, 1969.

[51] See, e.g., Chou En-lai speech in Pyongyang, New China News Agency dispatch, April 7, 1970

By the end of 1970, Peking was concerned over what appeared to be the movement of American policy toward "two Chinas" [52] and the concern remained acute into the spring of 1971. On the other hand, Peking was aware that it benefited, in the United States as elsewhere, from a substantial body of opinion anxious for better relations with China and prepared to believe that its own government's policy was the main obstacle to such an improvement. An exercise in "people's diplomacy" accordingly seemed called for, and one was in fact conducted with the skill for which Chou En-lai is famous. Even so, Peking waited for Washington's removal in mid-March 1971 of the remaining travel restrictions; these had been resented as humiliating and discriminatory even though Peking recognizes no reciprocal obligation to allow its citizens to travel to the United States or anywhere else.

Even more important, Peking apparently drew from the irresolute American handling of the Laotian crisis of February-March 1971, and especially from the noninvolvement of American ground forces, the conclusion that the United States was losing its nerve and was sincere in seeking relaxation of tension in Asia.[53] It believed that by the use of carefully orchestrated propaganda and diplomacy, the United States might be maneuvered into making important concessions while Peking's relations with the Soviet Union remained in their current state of essential deadlock. In early April, China issued the famous invitation to the American table tennis team, and soon afterward to a series of American correspondents, to visit China. During the next several weeks, in a highly secret manner that may have involved Romanian President Ceausescu, the celebrated visit of Dr. Henry Kissinger to Peking (July 9-11) was arranged.

The American interest at that stage in better relations with Peking was based on an overriding concern, for domestic political reasons to a large extent, for a settlement in Indochina and on a belief that Peking could be helpful in that regard if it would; at the minimum, American contacts with China might put Hanoi under pressure to be more reasonable at Paris. In addition, there was of course a broader American desire to accelerate military disengagement from Asia, as well as an interest in

---

[52] Cf. "Welcome the Establishment of Diplomatic Relations Between China and Canada," New China News Agency, October 15, 1970; "Welcome the Establishment of Diplomatic Relations Between China and Italy," New China News Agency, November 8, 1970.

[53] Cf. Ross Terrill in *Washington Post,* July 22, 1971.

using China if possible to help balance the Soviet Union and Japan, and a hope that Peking might be induced to refrain from applying pressures on its Asian neighbors, including Taiwan.[54]

The Chinese interest with respect to the United States was defined in a series of interviews given by Chou En-lai to visiting foreigners beginning in April 1971. Chou's position was that the United States must withdraw from all of Indochina—not merely Vietnam, as Hanoi and the National Liberation Front were currently demanding—before other issues could be settled. The basis was supposedly to be the National Liberation Front's demands—rather than a revived Geneva Conference, to which Hanoi was evidently opposed. Peking knew of course that the Nixon administration was anxious to disengage from Vietnam. The other crucial problems that Chou identified were Taiwan and Japan (with the related problem of tension between North and South Korea). To a considerable extent, Chou's position on the Taiwan question was consistent with earlier Chinese demands. The United States must withdraw all its forces and bases from Taiwan and the Taiwan Strait, recognize Taiwan as part of China and its "liberation" as a purely internal Chinese matter, withdraw recognition from the Republic of China, and in no way pursue a "two Chinas" policy or promote the Taiwan independence movement. To this Chou added an explicit demand, one apparently not made before in public, for the abrogation of the "invalid" security treaty between the United States and the Republic of China on Taiwan. Implicitly at least, the United States was also expected to help Peking cope with the alleged problem of Japanese remilitarization: for one thing, a peace treaty (on Communist terms) among the former belligerents in the Korean War would help to eliminate a traditional springboard for Japanese adventures on the Asian continent. (Chinese demands on the United States with respect to Korea, especially one for complete American military withdrawal from South Korea, are also undoubtedly intended as a means of cultivating Peking's rather delicate relations with Pyongyang.) Only after significant progress had been made toward the satisfaction of these demands would Peking be willing to establish diplomatic relations with the United States. According to Chou, Chinese representation in the United Nations was regarded as a separate question, a matter of princi-

---

[54] Cf. Kenneth Crawford in *Washington Post*, July 26, 1971. On the bad state of American-Japanese relations, mainly on account of economic issues, see Richard Halloran and Takashi Oka in *New York Times*, August 4, 1971.

ple that it would be both undignified and unnecessary to bargain over. Chou repeated Peking's familiar position that it would not sit in the United Nations if Taipei remained in it. Peking is apparently not prepared, however, to make the emerging American "two Chinas" policy for the United Nations an occasion for withdrawing its invitation to President Nixon or otherwise endangering the trend toward improvement in its relations with the United States. Virtually nothing was said about the Soviet aspect of the Sino-American relationship, although it was real enough; presumably Peking did not wish to provoke Moscow or weaken its hand in dealing with the United States by a display of concern over its Soviet problem. Peking probably believed that growing contacts with the United States would be useful, if not necessarily sufficient, in themselves, as a restraint on Moscow.[55]

It is reasonably certain that the Chou-Kissinger talks proceeded very much along the lines just indicated. The United Nations and Soviet questions do not appear to have been extensively discussed; one indication of this is that no specialist on either question accompanied Kissinger. The emphasis in all probability was on Taiwan and Indochina, and of course on the projected visit of President Nixon at some time before May 1972. Each side clearly realized the width of the gap separating its position from the other's, but each was eager, for reasons already indicated, to begin exploring the possibilities for narrowing the gap.[56]

---

[55] Probably the most important of Chou's recent interviews have been the following: one of June 21, 1971, with three American journalists (see Robert Keatley in *Wall Street Journal*, June 23, 1971; Seymour Topping in *New York Times*, June 23, 1971; William Attwood in *Washington Post*, June 26, 1971); one of July 19, 1971, with a group of American students (see John Burns in *New York Times*, July 21, 1971; in *Washington Post*, July 21, 1971; in *Christian Science Monitor*, July 22, 1971; see also *New York Times*, July 29, 1971); and one of August 5, 1971, with James Reston (transcript in *New York Times*, August 10, 1971).

These press accounts of the second interview are based on summaries of the conversation given by spokesmen for the students and (mainly in the last case) on an apparently authentic transcript later circulated by the students and available through the Pacific News Service in San Francisco. Chou evidently intended to be taken as speaking unofficially to the students, since he said that he would probably make some "erroneous remarks." The Foreign Ministry nevertheless authorized the circulation of his remarks, apparently in this form. For general comments on the Chinese position with respect to the United States see Ted Szulc in *New York Times*, August 7, 1971; and James Reston in *New York Times*, August 8, 1971.

[56] For comment on the Chinese position see Edgar Snow, "China Will Talk from a Position of Strength," *Life*, July 30, 1971, pp. 22-24, 26; for comment on the American position see President Nixon's press conference of August 4, 1971, in *New York Times*, August 5, 1971.

Since the Kissinger mission, President Nixon has stated that the United States will not abandon Taiwan or its other Asian allies, although in fact all of them, especially Japan and of course the Republic of China, have been affected in various ways by recent developments in Sino-American relations. Secretary of State William P. Rogers indicated support (on August 2, 1971) for "two Chinas" in the United Nations— a situation that Peking continues to reject and that Taipei has opposed in the past.[57] On the other hand, the Nixon administration has stopped flights over China by SR-71 reconnaissance aircraft [58] and has apparently decided against moving nuclear weapons from Okinawa to Taiwan.[59]

On the Chinese side, Peking obviously approves of most of President Nixon's performance to date but continues to pepper the United States with propaganda blasts in addition to its more serious demands. The elderly second level Chinese official, Kuo Mo-jo, told the Canadian opposition leader, Robert L. Stanfield, that President Nixon must make concessions before coming to China if he wishes his visit to have any useful result.[60] In his 1971 Army Day speech, Chief of Staff Huang Yung-sheng insisted that [61]

> the United States must withdraw all its military personnel and military installations from Taiwan Province and the Taiwan Straits area. . . . U.S. imperialism must completely withdraw its aggressor troops from Indochina, the southern part of Korea, the Philippines, Thailand and all other countries and regions which it has occupied and stop its interference in the internal affairs of the peoples in the Middle East and the Arab people as well as the peoples of Asia, Africa and Latin America.

There are indications, however, that extreme positions like Kuo's and Huang's are mainly propaganda and bargaining devices, and that Peking's actual negotiating position is somewhat more flexible. That flexibility is more likely to be evident with respect to Indochina, and therefore at the expense of Hanoi rather than with respect to Taiwan, where Peking considers that a major question of principle and national interest is involved and that it must do something to head off the threat

---

57 Secretary Rogers' press conference in *New York Times,* August 3, 1971.
58 William Beecher in *New York Times,* July 29, 1971.
59 Richard Halloran in *New York Times,* July 20, 1971.
60 John Burns in *Washington Post,* July 27, 1971; *New York Times,* July 31, 1971.
61 New China News Agency dispatch, July 31, 1971; for comment see James Reston in *New York Times,* August 2, 1971.

of "two Chinas." Indeed, Peking, which knows that President Nixon is anxious not to see his visit to China be canceled or fail, may try to capitalize on this attitude to extract major concessions on Taiwan in exchange for a modification of Peking's current demands with respect to Indochina.[62]

It is not hard to see why the Soviet Union should be concerned, as it has been since about 1966, over any prospect for a significant improvement in Sino-American relations.[63] Concrete Sino-American cooperation against the Soviet Union, if it should develop, would be so obviously disadvantageous to Moscow that the point needs no elaboration, and Sino-American cooperation on other issues would always hold the possibility of turning against the Soviet Union. Even short of that, the spectacle of the Soviet Union's former principal ally not only breaking with it but preferring a détente with the Soviet Union's principal adversary would raise, from Moscow's point of view, the gravest ideological and political problems and would pose a serious threat to what remains of the Soviet Union's alliance system. In short, any significant improvement in Sino-American relations, by whichever side it is initiated, will tend to alarm the Soviet Union; similarly any improvement in Soviet-American relations will tend to alarm Peking. At least, this is true under present conditions. Given these conditions, recent experience suggests that the United States may benefit in terms of its relations with the third party from a modest improvement in its relations with either China or the Soviet Union—an improvement, that is, that falls short of suggesting actual collaboration to the disadvantage of the third party.

## American Interests and Options

The United States has a major interest in stability in eastern Asia, and it appears that stability is best served when the Sino-Soviet-American relationship is an approximately equilateral triangle—that is, when no two are in a state of serious tensions, and when no two are close enough to seem to constitute a threat to the third. Accordingly, the United States ought to seek (as it has sought) to improve its relations with both the Soviet Union and China more or less simultaneously, but it ought also

---

[62] Cf. Ian Stewart in *New York Times,* August 4, 1971.

[63] For indications of Soviet concern over "ping pong diplomacy," see R. Moskvitin, "The United States and the PRC—The Diplomacy of Smiles,' " *New Times,* no. 13 (March 26, 1971), pp. 28-29; A. Nadezhdin, "Metamorphoses of Peking Diplomacy,"*New Times,* no. 22 (May 1971), pp. 22-23.

to accept and even welcome a comparable improvement in Sino-Soviet relations. There appears to be little chance at present of any of the three relationships suddenly turning into an entente—an outcome that is regarded for the purposes of this analysis as undesirable. The point is that, for the sake of stability, it would be best if none of the three trends (in Soviet-American relations, in Sino-American relations, and in Sino-Soviet relations) progressed at a pace markedly different from the other two.

Obviously such a situation is not within the unilateral power of the United States to ensure, but it can at least avoid actions that might tend toward the opposite. To a considerable extent this is what the Nixon administration has done, for example, in refusing to take sides in the Sino-Soviet dispute or to try to manipulate it. Where the Nixon administration can be seriously faulted in this connection, in the writer's opinion, is in its refusal in 1969 to take a clear public stand against Soviet bullying of China, as the Johnson administration had done a year earlier in the case of Soviet bullying of Romania (but not, unfortunately, of Czechoslovakia). Soviet humiliation and browbeating, to say nothing of military defeat, of China would be seriously detrimental to balance and stability in the Far East, and clear political opposition to it would be reasonably effective on past evidence, without the need for crude threats or military action in all probability. Such a course of action would not really be to side with China in the Sino-Soviet dispute but to serve an American interest that is as old as the Open Door: the principle that China ought not to be dominated or bullied by a foreign power.

Certainly a Machiavellian effort at manipulation of the Sino-Soviet dispute would be unlikely to have a positive payoff and should be avoided; indeed, it is not easy to see how it could be attempted. President de Gaulle's recognition of Peking in January 1964 was in part an anti-Soviet move, and it has brought France little benefit in this or any other respect. West German Finance Minister Franz Josef Strauss has cited the Sino-Soviet dispute as a reason why he considers it unnecessary to accept the Soviet-imposed status quo in Central Europe, but he has not, to the writer's knowledge, publicly advocated trying to manipulate the Sino-Soviet dispute.[64] Willy Brandt, while West German foreign minister,

---

[64] Franz Josef Strauss, *Challenge and Response: A Programme for Europe*, New York: Atheneum, 1970 (German edition published in 1968), pp. 75-76.

explicitly repudiated any idea of siding with China in order to gain leverage on the Soviet Union.[65]

In short, rather than the essentially negative strategy of trying to exploit the Sino-Soviet dispute, the proper policy for the United States is to promote its own positive interests in the Far East as elsewhere. This is the best way both to have the necessary strength for coping with the Soviet Union and China as adversaries if that should be necessary and for bargaining constructively with them whenever possible and desirable. Although this may appear to be a platitude when stated in such general terms, its implications need not be banal in practice. For example, the Nixon Doctrine, whose most important feature is a substantial reduction of the American military presence in the Far East and the Western Pacific, threatens to reduce the United States' influence in the region. This may happen not merely through the reduction of our actual power to a level insufficient to balance that of the Soviet Union and China but through the creation of the impression of being a power that does not know its own mind and has lost its nerve on account of its experience in Vietnam. To swing from excessive militarization of a local war to precipitate withdrawal, as the United States now appears to be doing, is not a manifestation of sound policy toward a region where persistence is what gets results.

Among the unfortunate consequences of American withdrawal may well be the passing of all of Indochina to Hanoi's control; competitive Chinese activity in some such area as Thailand; and intensified Soviet efforts in various parts of Asia to keep abreast of China.

Conversely, had a strategy been adopted that involved an effort in Vietnam more appropriate to a high level counterinsurgency operation than to a conventional war, the result might have been a persistence of self-confidence on the part of the United States sufficient to permit support for China against the Soviet Union when it was needed and deserved in 1969. There seems little chance now for the United States to reach the position it should have attained in 1969 with respect to the Sino-Soviet dispute, and no chance at all for it to adopt the strategy with respect to Vietnam that it ought to have adopted in 1965. But the United States could at least refrain from withdrawing from areas, like South Korea, where it seems politically unwise to do so and it could decide to render China at least declaratory support of the kind it failed

[65] Boris Meissner, ed., *Die deutsche Ostpolitik, 1961-1970: Kontinuität und Wandel,* Köln: Verlag Wissenschaft und Politik, 1970, p. 325.

to give in 1969, if China should again be faced with comparable Soviet pressures. Such a posture would of course prevent the United States from satisfying Peking's demands with respect to Taiwan, Indochina, Japan, and Korea, except to the limited extent that it may prove possible to do so in a way compatible with the American interest in avoiding changes in the Far Eastern balance of an undesirably destabilizing kind. The opportunities for American initiatives or responses of a more constructive kind are few at present; one of them appears to exist, along the lines just indicated, in the area of the Sino-Soviet dispute.

# Chronology

**1954**

October      Mao raises the problem of Mongolia with **Khrushchev**.

**1957**

January      Chou En-lai raises question of Mongolia with **Bulganin**.

**1959**

January 23      Peking formally repudiates the McMahon Line.

September 9      Soviet Union deplores Sino-Indian border tension.

**1962**

Spring      Tension along border between Sinkiang and Soviet Central Asia.

October–
November      Sino-Indian border war.

December 12      Khrushchev publicly taunts China with its failure to press territorial claims against the "imperialist" powers.

**1963**

March 8      Peking says the "unequal treaties" imposed on China by tsarist Russia may have to be revised.

May      Moscow proposes talks on the border question.

**1964**

February 23      Sino-Soviet border talks begin in Peking.

July 10      Mao, in interview with a Japanese delegation, accuses the Soviet Union of taking territory from China and Japan, as well as from other countries, since 1945.

September 2      Soviet editorial rejects Chinese territorial claims.

November      Post-Khrushchev Soviet leadership offers Peking an accommodation.

**1965**

February      Escalation of Vietnam war.

## 1965

| February 11 | Kosygin, in Peking, repeats offer with emphasis on "united action" over Vietnam. |
| April | Sino-Soviet agreement on rail transit facilities for Soviet military equipment bound for Vietnam. |
| September 3 | Lin Piao, in *Long Live the Victory of People's War!* restates the Maoist case against the Soviet Union in the context of the Chinese strategic debate over Vietnam. |
| September 29 | Chinese Foreign Minister Chen Yi refers to the possibility of a Sino-Soviet war. |
| November 11 | Peking formally rejects "united action." |

## 1966

| January | Soviet Union renews its alliance with Mongolia and begins to reinforce its military units stationed there. |
| January-February | Moscow circulates its "secret letter" against Peking. |
| March 23 | Peking announces its refusal of the Soviet invitation to send a delegation to the CPSU's Twenty-third Congress. |
| December | CPSU Central Committee Plenary Session apparently considers forcible action against China in the context of the Cultural Revolution. |
| August 21 | The Soviet Union invades Czechoslovakia. |
| August 23 | Peking denounced the Soviet invasion of Czechoslovakia. |

## 1968

| September 12 | Albania withdraws from the Warsaw Pact. |
| September 16 | Peking alleges Soviet overflights over Manchurian territory. |
| October | Victor Louis visits Taiwan. |
| October 13-31 | Mao, at CCP Central Committee's Twelfth Plenary Session, reportedly describes the Soviet Union as China's major enemy. |
| November 25 | Peking proposes resumption on February 20, 1969, of ambassadorial talks with the United States. |
| November-December | Chinese Chief of Staff Huang Yung-sheng visits Albania. |

**1969**

| | |
|---|---|
| January 25 | Mao, after several weeks' absence from public view, presides at a military rally. |
| January 27 | Chinese press begins a campaign against the Nixon administration. |
| Mid-February | Soviet forces intensify patrolling along the Far Eastern sector of the Sino-Soviet frontier. |
| February 19 | Peking cancels the session of the Sino-American ambassadorial talks scheduled for February 20. |
| Late February | "Minicrisis" over West Berlin. |
| March 2 | Sino-Soviet clash on Chenpao (Damansky) Island in the Ussuri River. |
| March 15 | Second clash on Chenpao (Damansky). |
| March 17 | Brezhnev denounces China at a Warsaw Pact meeting in Budapest. |
| March 21 | Kosygin tries to telephone Peking to discuss easing of the crisis. |
| March 22 | Peking's reply insists on use of normal diplomatic channels. |
| March 29 | Soviet government statement rejects the basic Chinese position on the border question and demands "consultations." |
| April 1-24 | CCP Ninth Congress; Lin Piao reaffirms Chinese position but makes it clear that Peking is not actually demanding the return of territories ceded under the "unequal treaties." |
| April 11 | Moscow proposes that 1964 border "consultations" be resumed April 15. |
| April 26 | Moscow proposes Khabarovsk as the site for annual talks on border river navigation; Peking accepts on May 11. |
| Mid-May | Peking begins to send ambassadors back to their posts. |
| May 24 | Chinese statement rejects Soviet demand of April 11, restates the basic Chinese position, and avoids naming a date for talks. |
| June 7 | Brezhnev denounces China and proposes a "system of "collective security" in Asia at international Communist conference in Moscow. |

**1969**

June 13   Soviet statement demands "consultations" within 2-3 months.

June 18   Sino-Soviet talks on border river navigation begin.

July 8    Sino-Soviet clash near Khabarovsk.

July     Nixon administration begins gradual easing of trade and travel restrictions on mainland China; announcement of Nixon Doctrine.

Early August  President Nixon visits Romania.

August 6   Threatening *Red Star* article by new commander of Soviet Far Eastern forces, V. F. Tolubko.

August 13   Sino-Soviet clash near western border of Sinkiang.

August 28   Threatening editorial in *Pravda*.

September 3  Death of Ho Chi Minh.

September 5  U.S. Under Secretary of State Elliot Richardson states American unwillingness to take sides in the Sino-Soviet dispute.

September 10 Tass charges China with 488 border violations, June to mid-August.

September 11 Chou-Kosygin talks in Peking.

September 16 Chinese National Day slogans suggest unwillingness to compromise. Threatening article by Victor Louis.

September 18 Peking sends message to Moscow proposing ceasefire and troop withdrawal.

October 6   Having received no reply, Peking sends another such message.

October 7   Peking announces agreement to hold border negotiations in Peking in near future.

October 8   Chinese statement rejects and "refutes" Soviet statement of June 13.

October 20  Border negotiations begin.

Mid-December Principal Soviet negotiators return to Moscow. Peking indicates increased interest in resuming ambassadorial talks with the United States.

## 1970

| | |
|---|---|
| January 2 | Chief Soviet negotiator returns to Peking. |
| January 5 | Sino-Soviet border talks resume. |
| January 20 | Session of Sino-American ambassadorial talks held at Warsaw. |
| February 20 | Session of Sino-American ambassadorial talks held at Warsaw. |
| May 18 | Peking cancels a session of the Sino-American ambassadorial talks scheduled for May 20, on account of the Cambodian crisis. |
| May 20 | Mao issues a statement denouncing the United States for its intervention in Cambodia. |
| July 1 | President Nixon says better Sino-American relations would help the United States to cope with the Soviet Union. |
| September 12 | Peking denounces the Soviet-West German treaty. |
| October 10 | V. S. Tolstikov, the new Soviet ambassador to China, arrives in Peking. |
| November 23 | Liu Hsin-ch'üan, the new Chinese ambassador to the Soviet Union, arrives in Moscow. |
| November 23 | Sino-Soviet trade agreement signed. |
| December 22 | *People's Daily* denounces Gierek regime and Soviet policy toward Poland. |

## 1971

| | |
|---|---|
| Late February-early March | Crisis over Laos. |
| March 15 | United States removes all travel restrictions on mainland China. |
| April | American table tennis team and correspondents visit China. |
| June 1-9 | Ceausescu visit to China. |
| June 8-15 | Tepavac visit to China. |
| June 10 | United States reduces trade restrictions against mainland China almost to level applying to the Soviet Union. |

**1971**

| | |
|---|---|
| July 9-11 | First Kissinger visit to China. |
| July 15 | President Nixon announces he will visit China before May 1972. |
| August 9 | Soviet-Indian friendship treaty. |
| August 17 | Publication in *People's Daily* of article apparently aimed at Lin Piao. |
| September 3 | Four-power agreement on West Berlin. |
| September 11 | Chou En-lai apparently begins purge of Lin Piao. |
| October 5 | Second Kissinger visit to China is announced. |
| October 20-26 | Kissinger in China. |
| October 25 | Peking is voted into the United Nations. |

# Selected Bibliography

## PRIMARY SOURCES

### 1. Chinese

"Down with the New Tsars!" *People's Daily* and *Red Flag*, March 4, 1969.
"Heighten Vigilance, Defend the Motherland," *People's Daily, Red Flag, Liberation Army Daily*, August 1, 1970.
*In Refutation of Modern Revisionism*, Peking: Foreign Languages Press, 1958.
"Leninism or Social Imperialism?" *People's Daily, Red Flag, Liberation Army Daily*, April 22, 1970.
Lin Piao. *Long Live the Victory of People's War!* Peking: Foreign Languages Press, 1965.
————. Report to the Ninth Party Congress, April 1, 1969 (text released by New China News Agency, April 27, 1969).
"Long Live the Victory of the Proletariat—in Commemoration of the Centenary of the Paris Commune," *People's Daily, Red Flag, Liberation Army Daily*, March 18, 1971.
"No Sign Yet of Progress in Sino-Soviet Border Talks," *Ta Kung Pao Weekly Supplement* (Hong Kong), November 6-12, 1969.
*The Polemic on the General Line of the International Communist Movement*, Peking: Foreign Languages Press, 1965.
"Sino-Soviet Border Clashes," *Current Background* (American Consulate General, Hong Kong), no. 876 (April 11, 1969).
" 'Soviet Revisionist Social-Imperialism' or 'US-Soviet Collaboration,' " *Current Background*, no. 883 (June 26, 1969).

### 2. Soviet

"The Adventurist Course of Peking," *Pravda*, August 28, 1969.
Aleksandrov, I. (pseud.) "The Fiftieth Anniversary of the CCP," *Pravda*, July 1, 1971.
————. "Regarding Peking-Washington Contacts," *Pravda*, July 25, 1971.
Lvov, O. (pseud.). "The Political Maneuvers of the Mao Tse-tung Group," *Pravda*, January 11, 1969.
"Pseudorevolutionaries with the Mask Off," *Pravda*, May 18, 1970.
Tolubko, V. V. "The Glory of Heroes Lives," *Red Star*, August 6, 1969.

## RECENT WORKS ON SINO-SOVIET RELATIONS

Doolin, Dennis J., ed. *Territorial Claims in the Sino-Soviet Conflict: Documents and Analysis*, Stanford University: Hoover Institution, Studies 7, 1965.
Garthoff, Raymond L., ed. *Sino-Soviet Military Relations*, New York: Frederick A. Praeger, 1966.
Gitting, John, ed. *Survey of the Sino-Soviet Dispute: A Commentary and Extracts from the Recent Polemics, 1963-1967*, London: Oxford University Press, 1968.
Griffith, William E., ed. *The Sino-Soviet Rift*, Cambridge, Mass.: M.I.T. Press, 1964.
————. *Sino-Soviet Relations, 1964-1965*, Cambridge, Mass.: M.I.T. Press, 1967.
Halperin, Morton H., ed. *Sino-Soviet Relations and Arms Control*, Cambridge, Mass.: M.I.T. Press, 1967.

Krylov, G. M., ed. *Vneshniaia Politika KNR* (The Foreign Policy of the People's Republic of China), Moscow: International Relations Publishers, 1971.
Robinson, Thomas W. *The Sino-Soviet Border Dispute: Background, Development, and the March 1969 Clashes,* The RAND Corporation, RM-6171-PR, August 1970.
————. *The Border Negotiations and the Future of Sino-Soviet-American Relations,* The RAND Corporation, P-4661, August 1971.
Salisbury, Harrison E. *War Between Russia and China,* New York: Bantam, 1970.
Zagoria, Donald S. *The Sino-Soviet Conflict, 1956-1961,* Princeton University Press, 1962.

## RECENT WORKS ON U.S. POLICY TOWARD CHINA AND THE SINO-SOVIET DISPUTE

Barnett, A. Doak, and Reischauer, Edwin O., ed. *The United States and China: The Next Decade,* New York: Praeger, 1970.
Barnett, A. Doak. *A New U.S. Policy Toward China,* Washington: The Brookings Institution, 1971.
*China and U.S. Far East Policy, 1945-1966,* Washington: Congressional Quarterly Service, 1967.
Nixon, Richard M. "Asia After Viet Nam," *Foreign Affairs,* vol. 46, no. 1 (October 1967), pp. 111-125.
————. *U.S. Foreign Policy for the 1970's: A New Strategy for Peace,* Washington: U.S. Government Printing Office, 1970.
Wu, Yuan-li. *Communist China and the World Balance of Power,* Washington: American Enterprise Institute for Public Policy Research, 1971.

## NEWSPAPER AND PERIODICAL ARTICLES

Berton, Peter. "Background to the Territorial Issue," *Studies in Comparative Communism,* vol. 2, nos. 3 and 4 (July/October 1969), pp. 131-382.
Duevel, Christian. "Kosygin's Surprise Visit to Peking," *Radio Liberty Dispatch,* September 12, 1969.
Gwertzman, Bernard. Dispatches in *New York Times,* 1969-1971.
Herrick, R. Waring. "Brezhnev Builds a Bilateral Treaty Bulwark Against China," *Radio Liberty Dispatch,* May 20, 1970.
————. "Soviet Charges of Sino-U.S. Collusion Appraised," *Radio Liberty Dispatch,* July 9, 1970.
————. "Soviet Far East Policies Hamstrung by Fear of Irredentism," *Radio Liberty Dispatch,* March 23, 1971.
Hinton, Harold C. "Conflict on the Ussuri: A Clash of Nationalisms," *Problems of Communism,* vol. xx, nos. 1-2 (January-April 1971), pp. 45-59.
Institute for Strategic Studies, "The Military Balance Between the Soviet Union and China," in *The Military Balance 1970-1971,* London, 1970, pp. 99-101.
Kun, Joseph C. In Radio Free Europe Research Papers, 1970-1971.
Lowenthal, Richard. "Russia and China: Controlled Conflict," *Foreign Affairs,* vol. 49, no. 3 (April 1971), pp. 507-518.
Lü Yung-shu, "Preparations for War in Mainland China," a paper presented at the First Sino-American Conference on Mainland China, Taipei, Taiwan, December 1970.
Snow, Edgar. "Talks with Chou En-lai: The Open Door," *The New Republic,* March 27, 1971, pp. 20-23.
Wohl, Paul. Dispatches in *The Christian Science Monitor,* 1969-1971.
————. *Peking Expects Soviet Attack in October,* Investment Research, Equity Research Associates, New York, August 1969.